WE
KNOW

---

an invitation to explore our innate compassion

by Anne Mitchell
with illustrations by Suzanne King

Copyright © 2021 by Anne Mitchell.

All rights reserved. No portion of this book, except for brief review, may be reproduced, stored in a retrieval system, or transmitted in any form or by any means—electronic, mechanical, photocopying, recording, or otherwise—without the written permission of the author.

Author: Anne Mitchell
Illustrator & Book Designer: Suzanne King

ISBN-13: 978-1-7374438-2-7
Library of Congress Control Number: 2021924691

Published by:
Game B Press
Speedway, Indiana, USA
gamebpress.com

praise for WE KNOW

> Warning: This book may make you squirm. Or even change you.
>
> In *We Know*, Anne Mitchell bravely confronts a disturbing reality: we humans have decided that we have no choice but to eat animals, a decision that contradicts the innate love inside of us, that is, biophila, love for all living things. Our decision, however, is based on erroneous assumptions, which Mitchell identifies and challenges.
>
> As readers follow Mitchell back into childhood recollections of her love and compassion for animals—and her horror when she realized their fate—they will no doubt recall their own similar feelings. Mitchell writes with simplicity and clarity, presenting weighty ideas in easy-to-understand language—without "dumbing down" the content. Her emphasis on love, compassion, and reverence for life inspires us all to make life-affirming choices. And to guide children to do the same.
>
> — Pamela Wampler, Licensed Marriage and Family Therapist

I dedicate this book to all vegan activists working to create a compassionate world. May young activists receive the support they need to grow into their most compassionate, most powerful selves.

Table of Contents

Introduction	9
I Knew	15
The Lobsters	31
The Rabbits	39
The Chickens	47
The Cow	55
The Pig	63
The Deer	73
The Invitation	83
Conclusion	93
References	109
With Gratitude	115

> I think young people can really show us what compassion looks like, they can show us what empathy looks like. Think about it, man, our biggest insult, our biggest critique is that you're just so sensitive. We hear from comedians, we hear from everybody—they're just snowflakes, they're cupcakes, they're just too sensitive. What we're really doing is insulting them for being empathetic, we're insulting them for being compassionate because they want to see the many slivers of each individual free. Imagine that. I think we have much to learn from them if we would just give ourselves a moment of humility to listen a little more.
>
> — Jason Reynolds, author & Library of Congress' national ambassador for young people's literature [1]

I Knew
When I Was Five

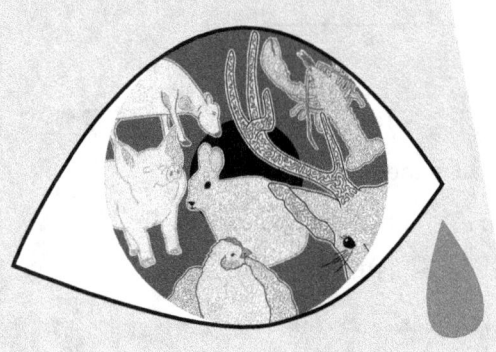

by Anne Mitchell
illustrated by Suzanne King

---

an invitation to explore
our innate compassion

We
KNOW

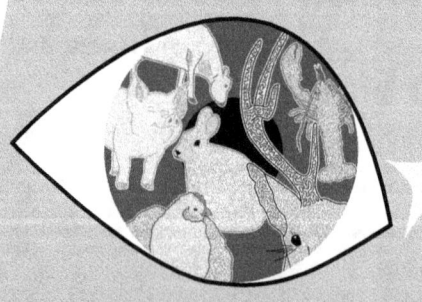

by Anne Mitchell
with illustrations by Suzanne King

INTRODUCTION

We Know **is both an invitation to explore an issue that goes largely unnoticed in our society and a companion book to a children's illustrated book we published in July 2021.**

The issue that is largely unnoticed in our society is the deep empathy and compassion human infants and toddlers hold for other living beings. We all find this empathy and compassion cute and heartwarming, but adults (parents, grandparents, teachers…) do little to support its development and actually quite a lot to overcome it.

With this book I hope to open that conversation in a different way than is usually discussed. I know there is a lot more here to uncover, analyze and discuss. My hope is to spark a new conversation.

The illustrated book is *I Knew When I Was Five*—for children, but its content is quite mature. It is about growing up and coming to terms with the manner in which human beings use non-human beings in a variety of ways in our everyday lives. It is the story of one five year old girl who grows up not understanding. She questions, often in her own head, how humans can possibly do the things we do to animals on a daily basis. It is about feeling like an outsider, even within her own family. About knowing, deep down in her heart and soul, that many aspects of daily life are wrong, deceptive and damaging, but having no idea about what to do with that knowledge because almost literally no one would discuss it, except to say:

"that's life,"

"get used to it,"

"that's normal, natural or necessary,"

"we have to eat, too,"

and other such platitudes that did not make sense.

This book is designed to illuminate all of that for the adults in the lives of the children who read that book. This book expands the conversation, to encourage adults to really think about how they learned about our use of animals and what their experience was. To encourage parents (and grandparents and teachers and aunts and uncles and babysitters…) to consider how the children they know are learning about these things. To consider how those children might be feeling and give them an opportunity to explore those feelings rather than simply indoctrinating them into the world view they themselves were indoctrinated into.

Indoctrinate *is* a strong word. Before rolling your eyes, think about the definition:

INTRODUCTION

indoctrinate   *verb*   / in-ˈdäk-trə-nāt /

indoctrinate somebody (with something) |
indoctrinate somebody (to do something) to force somebody to accept a particular belief or set of beliefs and not allow them to consider any others [2]

Most parents want their children to grow up to be critical thinkers, able to make their own decisions, based on careful analysis of whether something is true or false, good or bad, right or wrong. But what we really do is indoctrinate our children into using animals in all sorts of ways. Some are very obvious and open: for food, for clothing and furniture, for entertainment; others are hidden and not so obvious: shellac, dyes and inks, piano keys, tennis racquets, scientific experiments.

Don't we owe it to ourselves and our children—and the animals and the very planet—to actually think about this? To wonder: should we be using animals in all these ways? Do we *need* to use animals like this and this and this? What is the impact to us, to the earth, to the animals, because of our behavior?

I chose to write this book to help adults reflect on their own childhoods and think about how to talk about these subjects with the children in their lives. It feels important to tell the fuller stories behind the poem behind *I Knew When I Was Five*, both for myself and others.

My stories seem to remind others about their own stories of learning about how we use animals and remembering those stories helps people remember how they felt at the time. And remembering those feelings helps adults to think about, to be more attuned, to how the children they are with are feeling.

I hope that it goes without saying that we all want to live in a more compassionate, just, and sustainable world so that our children and their children are able to continue living on this miraculous planet. In order to do so, we all need to consider the lives of *all* living beings and figure out ways to live in harmony with each other.

Let's stop indoctrinating each other in harmful behaviors and start inspiring each other to create the world we actually want to live in. We can do this. Living compassionately *is* possible.

Please Note...

The words "humans" and "animals" will be used throughout this book, with the recognition that humans are animals and in this instance, the word "animals" actually refers to "non-human animals."

And another note: The stories told in chapters 2 through 7 are my memories of events that happened throughout my childhood and young(ish) adulthood. They are mine alone and I am under no delusion that others might have contradictory memories of those events. These are simply my memories. The names of places in these stories are generally real. The names of people in these stories have been changed to protect their privacy.

*I knew when I was five
And no one had to tell me.*

That killing is wrong.

*That every life
is precious
no matter who it is,
or what color, shape, size
— or species —
he or she or they
happen to be.*

I Knew

We know. I believe we are all born knowing. Knowing compassion, empathy, the value of life. The value of all life on earth. Humans, non-human mammals, birds, fish, insects, reptiles, plants, water, air. This knowledge is natural, instinctual, a part of our souls, our very cells. It is the natural state of human beings and the word biophilia describes this phenomenon:

> **biophilia** *noun* / bī-ō-ˈfī-lē-ə /
>
> **love of living things and nature, which some people believe humans are born with:** biophilia, the inborn affinity human beings have for other forms of life [3]

We come into this world KNOWING.

We marvel at the flower. We laugh at the antics of the squirrels. We are curious about the communities of ants we come across. We are in awe of the birds and butterflies as they fly around us. We cuddle with the cats and dogs and chickens and goats we are in contact with. We make friends with the cow and horse we meet. We watch our own reflections in the pond. We revel in the feel of the breeze on our face. We love everyone we meet. We love. As our natural way of being. As who we are. Until we no longer do.

We must learn to overcome our natural knowing, our natural loving selves—either by lived experience or indoctrination, or both. And almost every last one of us do overcome it to one degree or another. And the consequences of overcoming this knowing and loving have massive impacts on us, the other beings we share the planet with, and the planet herself. The terms *human supremacy, human exceptionalism, humanocentrisim,* and *anthropocentrism* are all used interchangeably to describe the idea that humans are superior to all other life forms and are separate from nature.

I will use the term **human supremacy** for most of this book. **Human supremacy is the sum of overcoming our natural state.**

We know that we are born knowing because of our own lived experiences and because of what we see in the children we know today. We remember that praying mantis we kept in a shoebox in our bedroom and how we cried when we woke one morning to find her dead. We remember being in awe of the fish swimming under the pier at our grandparents' lake house and how effortlessly they moved through the water. We remember when we first learned where our hamburger or chicken nuggets actually come from.

Or perhaps we remember when we had to answer our

children's questions about our food or clothing or furniture. How it felt like a betrayal to watch their face as they realized that the food you wanted them to eat had once been a living being who wanted to live. And still, you thought it was in their best interest to know, to know the "truth." This "truth" turns out to be one of the biggest lies of all time—the idea that humans can do to any other being anything they want just because they are human and the other is not. This is of course not the way we present this to the children in our lives the first time the subject comes up, at least not for most people. No, first we tell them that humans *have to* eat other animals to live and that eating animals is normal, natural and necessary.

This is the first of many lies we tell our children to support them in getting over their natural knowing.

We go on to tell children that being eaten is the purpose of many animals and that makes it okay to kill them and eat them. But where does this idea come from, that a pig or a chicken's (or any other animal in any culture) purpose in life is to be eaten by humans? We made that argument up from whole cloth. There is no animal whose purpose is to be eaten. Hard stop here. And the way that we share this idea is to show cows who happily give us their milk, pigs dancing near the barbecue pit, and chickens easily rolling out egg after egg as if they are happy to give their lives for humans. This could not be further from the truth.

Then we tell children that we treat the animals well until they die—another lie of massive proportions. Farmed animals today are the most abused, terrorized, mistreated beings of all time. There are virtually no laws requiring decent treatment of "livestock." Even the word is violent:

> "Livestock are distinguished from other animals by the fact that they're domesticated and raised for food or money—if you get wool, milk, meat, or eggs from animals, they're livestock. The word comes from the sense of stock that means 'supply for future use' or 'sum of money'; from the 1500s, this word was also used to mean 'movable property of a farm.'" [4]

The atrocities that humans commit against farmed animals is of epic proportions. We control every aspect of their lives from conception through death and most animals live in unending suffering. Think for a moment about why we can tour the donut shop and pick our own strawberries in the strawberry field but not ever see the slaughterhouse? Many U.S. states have laws prohibiting employees or activists from taking photos or videos of the treatment of animals on farms and at slaughterhouses. What are they hiding? What are we missing? Why do we pass this on to our own children without critical thought?

Most animals are born with some capacities: most large grazing animals like horses, giraffes or cows can walk within minutes of birth; many bird species can fly within a week of birth; reptiles can glide, walk and swim within hours of birth; infant fish can count to four and there is evidence of large number discrimination in baby fish as well. [5]

In other words, all babies are born with the ability to do some things, though we often think of babies, of any species, as quite incapable. So what are human babies capable of at birth or very soon after? Lots of things, according to scientists who study such questions.

Human babies can:
- smell and hear before birth so certainly can at birth
- see, although vision is still blurry early on
- recognize their mothers voices
- discriminate between their native language and others (French vs Russian, for example)
- recognize faces as opposed to other body parts or inanimate objects
- prefer their mothers faces to other faces
- prefer primate faces to other animal faces
- show empathy (by crying when they hear another infant in distress, at one day old)

Human babies share emotion with other infants within a day of birth. This is a big deal. Empathy has also been seen in primates, dogs, rats and other non-humans. Lobsters will walk along the ocean floor claw in claw with the older lobster leading the younger. It appears that we find empathy wherever we actually look for it. Our affinity for each other is natural and occurs in the very young—of any species.

DeLoache, Pickard, and LoBue explore this in *How very*

young children think about animals:

> "Recent evidence that humans are particularly attuned to animals right from the start comes from research conducted with newborns. Simion, Regolin, and Buff (2008) recently reported that newborns have a preference for looking at biological motion. In a series of studies, infants were shown pairs of point-light displays with both displays composed of the same number of lights. One display specified biological motion (a moving hen) and the other nonbiological (random) movement. The infants looked significantly longer at the biological than the random motion, suggesting that it was more coherent to them. (A preference for watching biological movement has also been documented in chickens.) Thus, enhanced attention to biological movement is common, both ontogenetically and phylogenetically." [6]

This paragraph is particularly interesting in that it notes that this preference for watching other beings is true for both human infants and in chickens, and one can imagine in most other living beings as well. And this makes sense as many species have evolved together and all parts of the ecosystem are necessary for proper functioning. We may not yet understand the full extent of each of our roles, our work, our purpose on this earth, but all species have a specific job to do in order to keep the whole working well. There are unlikely to be unnecessary actors though evolution continues and individual species will continue to evolve. Each of us, human or chicken or fish or whomever, is fascinated by the others on this earth as we each instinctively know that we are all bound together for the sake of the whole. And we know this at a very young age, perhaps at birth.

Again, biophilia is the word we use to describe this process.

"Biophilia" is an innate affinity of life or living systems. The term was first used by Erich Fromm to describe a psychological orientation of being attracted to all that is alive and vital. Wilson uses the term in a related sense when he suggests that biophilia describes "the connections that human beings subconsciously seek with the rest of life." He proposed the possibility that the deep affiliations humans have with other life forms and nature as a whole are rooted in our biology. Both positive and negative (including phobic) affiliations toward natural objects (species, phenomenon) as compared to artificial objects are evidence for biophilia.

Although named by Fromm, the concept of biophilia has been proposed and defined many times over. Aristotle was one of many to put forward a concept that could be summarized as "love of life." Diving into the term philia, or friendship, Aristotle evokes the idea of reciprocity and how friendships are beneficial to both parties in more than just one way, but especially in the way of happiness.

In the book *Children and Nature: Psychological, Sociocultural, and Evolutionary Investigations*, edited by Peter Kahn and Stephen

Kellert, the importance of animals, especially those with which a child can develop a nurturing relationship, is emphasized particularly for early and middle childhood. There is evidence in scientific studies and ample evidence in anecdotal stories, that children are drawn to animals with curiosity, empathy and compassion.

Consider this thought experiment: place a toddler, a young rabbit and an apple in a playpen together and we all know that the toddler and the bunny will share the apple and play together. And in the very, very odd and rare circumstance where the child or the rabbit tries to eat the other and play with the apple, everyone watching will be horrified.

In the case of an aggressive rabbit, the rabbit will be killed by adult humans. In the case of an aggressive toddler, the child will be removed from the area and psychological counseling will be sought. Biophilia certainly appears to be real and evident in humans and non-humans alike. We are all drawn to other life forms naturally and with kindness, curiosity, compassion, wonder and empathy.

Human supremacy is the idea that humans are superior to all other life forms, that other life forms are on earth to serve humans, that humans are really the only ones who matter. The philosophy of human supremacy counteracts biophilia quite handily, almost as if it were designed that way. Human supremacy is one of very few things humans appear to agree on. This is one of the few ideas that transcend race, gender, sexuality, politics, religion, economics — humans matter more than anyone else and humans get to do basically anything they want to other living beings.

While there are differences in the ways that groups use animals (Jains won't eat or wear animals but they produce and eat dairy; Hindus believe the cow is sacred and most are vegetarian, even meat eating Hindus won't eat beef; indigenous people thank the animals they kill for their sacrifice, yet they still kill them, eat them and use them; in the West dogs and cats are not considered food while they are in the East; the Massai cut the jugular veins of their cows regularly and drink the blood but won't eat the flesh, and the list incredibly goes on) there appear to be no countries or cultures that do not use animals in any way.

Crist explores the pervasive worldview of human supremacy in *Reimagining the human*:

"This worldview esteems the human as a distinguished entity that is superior to all other life forms and is entitled to use them and the places they live. The belief system of superiority and entitlement—or human supremacy—manifests in a range of anthropocentric commonplace assumptions, linguistic constructs, institutional regimes, and everyday actions of individual, group, nation-state, and corporate actors. For example, the human is invested with powers of life and death over all other beings and with the prerogative to control and manage all geographical space. The all-encompassing manifestation of the belief system of human supremacy is precisely what constitutes it as a worldview.

This worldview is not necessarily an explicitly articulated narrative. Rather, it forms the tacit postulate from which people source meaning and justification to disregard virtually any limitation of action or way of life in the ecosphere and toward nonhumans. Human supremacy is the underlying big story that normalizes the trends of more, and the consequent displacements and exterminations of nonhumans—as well as of humans who oppose that worldview. In this context, it is crucial to recognize that human supremacy is neither culturally nor individually universal, nor is it derived in any straightforward way from human nature. However, western civilization has elaborated its most forceful, long-standing expression, and through the West's ascendancy the influence of this worldview has spread across the globe." [7]

Read this again: "In this context, it is crucial to recognize that human supremacy is neither culturally nor individually universal, nor is it derived in any straightforward way from human nature."

And yet it is a worldview that encompasses just about every culture on earth. As Kelch notes in *Cultural Solipsism, Cultural Lenses, Universal Principles, And Animal Advocacy*:

"Indeed, the 'universality of human violence against animals' is remarkable." [8]

While arguments can be made that specific cultures (indigenous cultures around the globe for example) recognize that the natural world and the animals that inhabit that world are sentient, valuable and finite and therefore must be used with respect and thoughtfulness for the future, all human cultures appear to use animals in some way. These are learned behaviors. They are not part of human nature. There have always been individual people who warned against the exploitation of animals and the natural world going back further than the written word. Pythagorus appears to be the first human to actively argue that animals are sentient and deserve protection in (or about) 530 BCE. The idea of respecting and protecting animals is quite well established. Not embraced, but well established. [9]

People seem to have run amok killing animals and destroying habitat on an unimaginable scale, but even the act of killing wild animals, thanking them for their sacrifice and only killing a few animals while protecting their habitat, is still disrespectful to the animals. It may be respectful enough to the earth to not cause massive extinctions and global warming, but it is still violent and disrespectful towards the animals. And altogether unnecessary at this point in time.

Humans have no need to eat animal flesh or secretions or use their body parts for anything or use their strength for anything. Alternatives for every use of animals already exist or have been developed by humans.

Another point worth considering is that our taste buds are developed over time and in context of the culture we live in and the foods we find acceptable and delectable are learned. Consider the fact that children eat what their parents and other adults give them to eat. When children won't eat a certain food, parents work hard to get them to eat that food. While all individuals are just that—individuals—and there are foods that our families love that we do not, our preference in food is learned from our family and then our community. Some of us are adventurous in the food we eat and will try anything. Others stick pretty close to the foods of our childhoods. But our taste buds are developed, trained, habituated, to like the foods we eat rather than to eat the food we like.

This explains why there are such diverse food styles across the world and almost everyone who grows up in that place, loves the food, no matter their ethnicity. A white child from England growing up in Thailand (in a Thai family, eating hot Thai food) will grow up to love Thai food with all its heat and will find traditional English fish and chips weird or bland or whatever. Different places and peoples have created cuisines that took advantage of their local biodiversity in both plants and animals—so there are vegetable curries with cheese dishes in India; rice, vegetables and fish in Japan; corn, beans and hot peppers in Central America; goats and sheep eaten primarily in the middle east, while cows are eaten in Europe and the US and almost any animal is eaten in China, including domestic cats and dogs.

There may have been reasons for those food choices in the past, but today we can grow food in many more places, including indoors, and move it around the world where we need it most. We don't have to rely on what we did in the past. Winter does not mean that we can't eat fruits and vegetables. We can freeze, can and dry food with ease. We can fly or ship food where it is needed. We are no longer bound by the rules of the past.

Further complicating the matter is that certain foods are hard-wired into our biology to help us stay alive. Fruit is really good for us and only available for short times of the year in most places, so our taste buds evolved to love sweets. We evolved to love fat so that we would eat fatty foods like nuts and seeds, especially in the fall of the year to give us added protection against the cold of winter. Today those evolutionary developments actually work against us as food companies use those hard-wired evolutionary hacks to create food that hits the "bliss-point" and keeps us coming back for more. (See *Salt, Sugar, Fat* by Michael Moss and *The Pleasure Trap* by Doug Lisle).

The cool thing about the fact that our taste buds are trained to like the food we like is that we can re-train our taste buds to like food that is good for us, good for the planet and compassionate to the animals! Taste buds regenerate every two weeks so it doesn't take that long to get used to a new taste. [10]

Though in all honesty, our memories and our noses also remember the old tastes, so it does take a small amount of work to totally change the things we like. But it *is* possible.

To sum up, we are born with biophilia, a natural tendency to love and respect non-human animals; our taste buds are trained and habituated to like the foods we are told to eat; and human supremacy is a learned belief that has developed over thousands of years but has no basis in science and has proven highly damaging to our planet and the other beings we share this planet with. It is time to rethink how we think about our role on the earth and possible futures.

Chapters 2 through 7 tell the story of how our culture attempts to overcome our natural empathy and compassion for other animals with the misguided belief of human supremacy and the training of our taste buds.

These stories showcase how one child/adult experienced

this phenomena with the hope that parents will think deeply about how they want to raise their children and older children who read these stories might find the courage to hold onto their own truths.

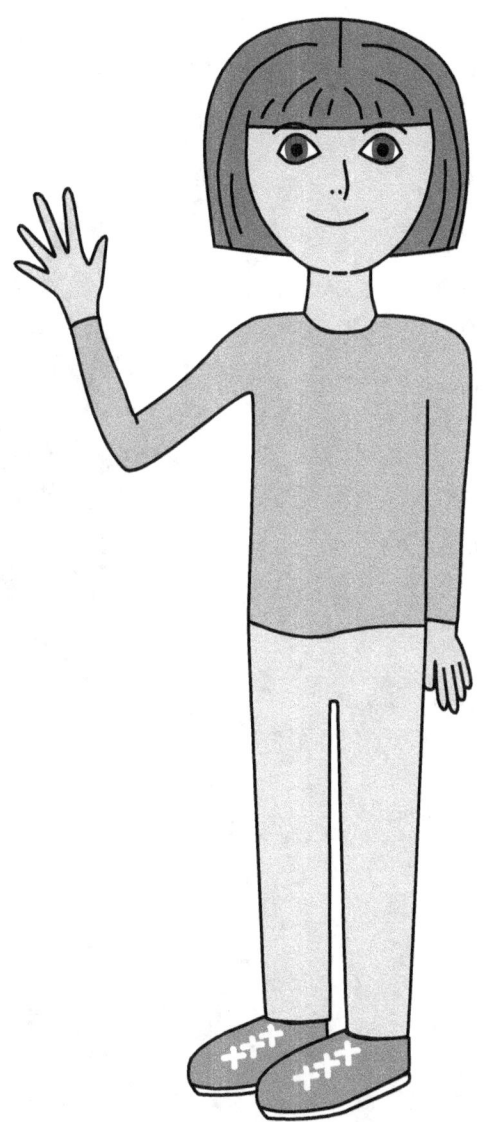

Lobsters have complex lives.

The women choose
whose babies they will have and
mothers carry their eggs
for 9 to 11 months
before they are born.

Lobsters grow old
and wise
and can live 100 years
and grow 3 feet long
and weigh 40 pounds.

I knew when I was five
and no one had to tell me

that boiling
a 1-pound, 5-year-old lobster
alive
to satisfy human tastebuds

was wrong.

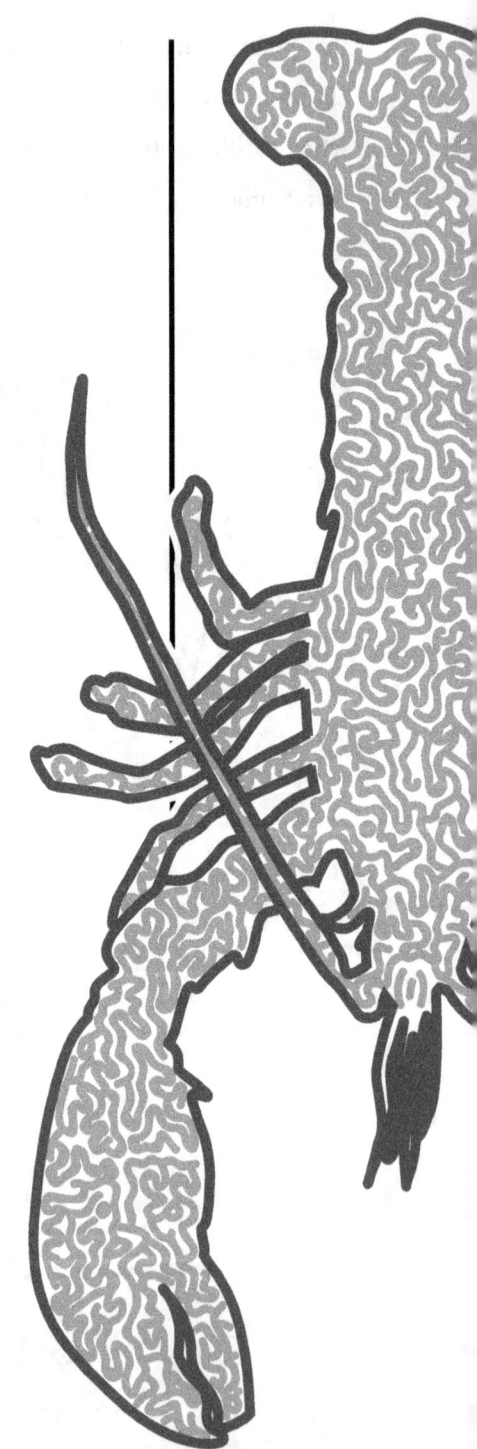

The Lobsters

My parents were born and raised in Massachusetts but moved to Cincinnati to follow a job in the 1950s. Our extended family continued to live in Massachusetts. My maternal grandparents had a summer house on Stiles Reservoir in Spencer, Massachusetts where we spent a month every summer with my father joining us for his two week work vacation. My grandfather bought three lots on the lake in 1926. He eventually built two summer houses on the lots, one on either side with the middle lot left unbuilt for picnic tables and a place to play and gather. My grandparents lived in one of the houses and one of my uncles, his wife, and their five sons and one daughter lived in the other. My mother was the oldest of four children and we were the oldest grandchildren. All of my cousins were my age or younger.

"Camp" was the way we referred to the summer house on the lake. The winter house was in Worcester, but we were hardly ever there and my memories of that house are very dim. We spent all of our time in Massachusetts on the lake at "camp."

We swam and boated and picked wild blueberries on blueberry island in the middle of the lake. My mother, her two brothers and one sister had all grown up on the lake, all learned to waterski, canoe, swim and fish. Using fish to eat and fertilize the garden was a common practice and no thought was ever given to the fish. I remember being uncomfortable when someone would catch a fish and want to put it back in the water but no one else seemed to even think about it. I don't remember ever voicing my concerns.

One of my very first memories of "camp" was when I was five. One of my uncles had a sailboat and lobster traps in Boston Harbor. On this particular day, I assume it was a weekend, he brought a number of freshly captured lobsters to camp. The adults set up a baby pool down by the lake and put the lobsters in the baby pool. A number of us were swimming and swinging and playing by the lake. We were told to leave the lobsters alone but of course we did not. We got sticks and poked at their claws and the lobsters grabbed the sticks and we spent the afternoon playing with the lobsters. I thought they were my new friends.

In the meantime, the adults were preparing dinner. There were big grills up closer to the house and near the picnic tables. This was a big area, the two large picnic tables easily sat 20 -30 people. The grilling area and picnic tables were in the shade of large trees and grass was sparse underfoot. This area was closer to the road and further from the lake and the land gently sloped down to the lake where there were more large trees including a rope swing hanging from one of the trees. Each house had a

THE LOBSTERS

dock and a boat and there was a raft between the two houses in the lake that we all swam to and played on.

I believe there was also corn on the cob, coleslaw and probably potato salad for dinner that day. There were large pots of water set to boiling on the grills. As dinner time approached, the adults came down to get the lobsters. I remember skipping beside them as we walked uphill to the grilling area. I did not anticipate what was about to happen. As we reached the grills, the adults dropped the lobsters into the boiling pots of water.

I could not believe it. I was heartbroken. I felt betrayed. I was horrified for the lobsters. I screamed and tried to pull the closest pot over to get the lobsters out.

My mother grabbed me before I touched the pot and dragged me away. I was spanked and yelled at and sent to my room in the house. I do not remember having any dinner that night. I do remember sobbing in my room alone that they killed "my" lobsters.

My mother told me to knock it off and left me alone. I had never felt so alone in my life.

The next day everyone talked about how delicious the lobsters were. I don't remember anyone taking me seriously or talking to me about my feelings or giving me any credibility at all for having these thoughts and feelings.

To this day I have never eaten lobster.

I wish I had made the connection between the lobster and all the other animals I was eating. Like most children today, I thought our food came from the store. Other than the wild blueberries we picked on Blueberry Island, all our food came from grocery stores, the produce truck that came by camp every week during the summer (just like the ice cream truck came by once a week) or the few restaurants we occasionally ate at. We did not grow any of our food, nor did any of my extended family.

I wish that one of the adults had seen fit to discuss this with me. I wish someone had noticed how distressed I was about this. I remember feeling so confused and so alone. I remember looking at all the adults with very different eyes after that day. I could not believe how cruel they could be. I could not believe they could kill and eat a living creature while talking and laughing and exclaiming with delight about how delicious the lobster was. I lost my trust in adults that day and I am not sure I ever recovered it.

How different might my life have been had I been taken seriously? How different might our world be if children were supported in their empathy and compassion rather than indoctrinated into this violence?

We have extended family reunions every five years and have since the 1980's. Twice they were held in the Midwest for various reasons. But in 2019, the reunion was held again at camp. I chose not to attend mostly because of the menu. It was full of animals and damn near nonexistent with anything nourishing. Chicken wings, pizza, hot dogs, hamburgers, chips, steamers, fish, steak, corn, and salad. I could not be present for the killing of the clams or the fish and did not choose to be near the other dead animals.

And I also chose not to go because I did not want to deal with the harassment I get for not eating animals. My cousins who grew up regularly eating lobster and fish they caught themselves are still eating and relishing eating those animals. They have posted photos or videos making fun of the live animals they are about to kill and eat. They seem to have no understanding of the harm they are doing to themselves, the planet or certainly not to the animals. And when I make a statement, I am again told to "lighten up" or something similar.

Men & Women

I am fully aware that many humans are uncomfortable using the words "man/men" and "woman/women" when referring to non-human animals. I find this very curious, especially when we are quite comfortable using the words "boy" and "girl" when referring to our domestic, pet animals. My dog or cat or horse can be such a "good girl" or "silly boy" or "clever girl" or "mischievous boy" but never do we use the words man or woman to discuss non-human animals. Chickens kept in backyards for egg production are often referred to as "our girls" or "the girls"... I don't think this has anything to do with

Men & Women, continued

gender or age or maturity and everything to do with power. I think this is a very complex issue (think about how we still use "girl" to refer to adult female humans but very rarely do we ever use the word "boy" to refer to adult male humans) and quite beyond the scope of this work. Suffice it to say that the use of the words man/men and woman/women when referring to adult non-human animals is done with intent, to invite the reader to think about how they emotionally experience those words in relation to non human animals. How do you feel? Why do you think that? What does that say about your belief system? What does this say about our society?

This issue is also, for me, connected to personhood. We, as a human society, have excluded non humans from having personhood status and the rights that come along with that status. Human children share some rights with adults but not all. Now there are U.S. corporations with legal personhood status [11] and two rivers in India [12] and a river in New Zealand [13] which all have legal personhood status, but non-human animals do not. I find this also very curious and worthy of introspection and consideration.

We appear comfortable acknowledging that non-human animals have gender, we talk about them as male and female, boy and girl, but are uncomfortable about using the words man and woman. I think this is worth thinking about, wondering about and grappling with.

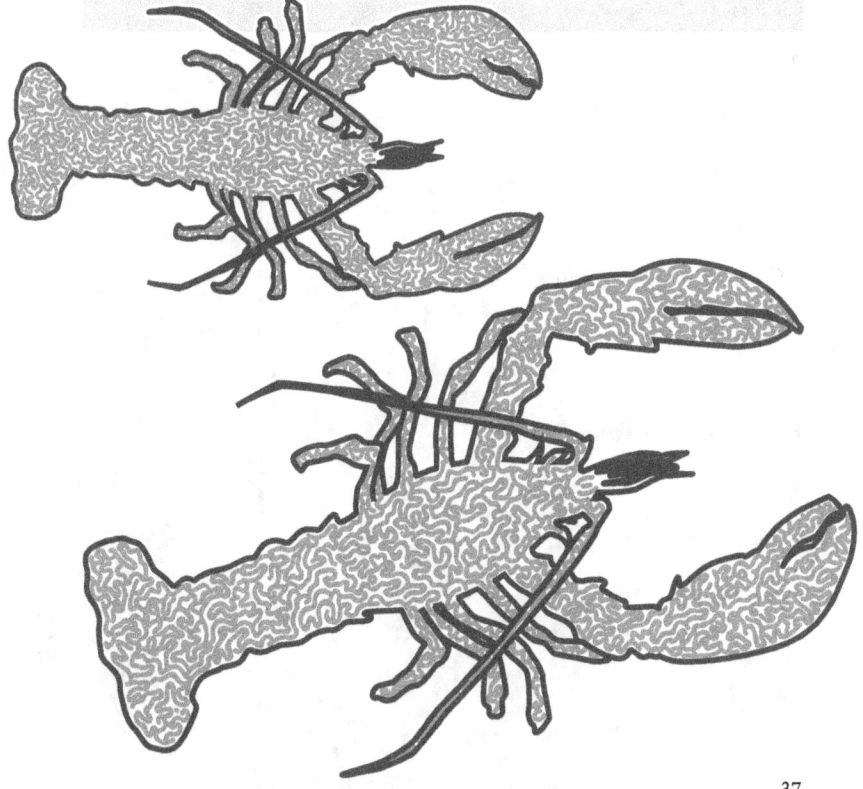

*Rabbits are gregarious
and live in communities
of up to 100 individuals.*

*They build houses
underground together
with separate rooms
for living and sleeping*

*and make lifelong friends
who play together,
calm each other
when stressed,
and nurture each other
when sick.*

*I knew when I was eight
and no one had to tell me*

*that killing and skinning
40 rabbits
so that one human
can wear a fur coat*

was wrong.

The Rabbits

Learning that animals were used to make clothing was something of a curiosity for me but turned to total revulsion as I understood that the animals were not shaved but were actually killed for their fur. When I first met Flint, the Thoroughbred who was kicked off the Detroit police force because he was too goofy and just wanted to have fun, I thought he was covered in "fur." His hair was a red, chestnut, kinda roan color. His mane and tail were quite long. In the Michigan winters he would grow a very thick coat which I could sink my hand into and feel the warmth of his skin. This was also true of Jill, the German Shepherd I grew up with. I recall telling Doris, who lived with Flint, that I loved his "fur" and she immediately corrected me and said that horses have hair, not fur, and that animals that have fur are used to make clothing, but horses are not. I found this interesting at the time and still wonder at her irritation with me about my misconception.

I believe she was trying to make sure I knew that horses

should not be used for human desires (beyond riding, showing, etc.). And somehow distinguishing between "hair" and "fur" was helpful to her in that regard.

I have since found out that the words "hair" and "fur" mean the same things. There is no scientific difference between the two. In usage, humans always have "hair," while many other mammals have fur, though sometimes we use the word "hair" as well, such as our references to cat hair and dog hair. So, my reference was not wrong. "Fur" is simply a made up word to allow humans to use the skin and hair of other mammals in ways we would never consider using human hair.

At about the same time I was getting to know Flint, my dad bought my mom a fur coat. This was a full length coat made of rabbit hair. It was brown and tan and cream and so incredibly soft. It was a big deal to my mother, who apparently had always wanted a fur coat. Her mother, my grandmother, had a mink stole. I was always freaked out to see that stole as it was made from one animal and the poor animal's head was still attached and the clasp was integrated into the dead mink's mouth. I think the clasp latched onto his/her own tail. It was truly awful. I rarely saw the stole, as we visited in the summer and there was no reason to bring the stole out. I think my grandmother also had a waist-length mink cape or something similar. I remember those to be dark brown and very shiny. I remember being sad that my mother wanted a fur coat at all. It seemed such a bad idea, even in the 1960's.

So my father bought the rabbit fur coat and I still remember the day they brought it home. My mother was so proud of that coat. She carefully took it out of the garment bag and tried it on in the living room, twirling around. It was just my dad, me and my little sister home to see this spectacle but still she was very happy about it. I got to touch the coat for just a minute and then I was told I could not touch it again without my mother being present. I was told the coat was very expensive and NOT A TOY. I was never to play with it or try it on. It was special and not for me.

My mother was not a fashionista. Her idea of makeup was putting on lipstick and a touch of rouge. She did not work outside the house and though they went to dinner often with friends and sometimes with my dad's business they were not into country clubs, theatre or showing off. So this whole rabbit fur coat came as a bit of a surprise. I was never allowed to play with my mother's clothing, jewelry or makeup, but it was just expected. There was no huge warning to stay away.

Which of course made this coat very interesting to my eight-year-old self. I had to understand what was so special about this coat. I had to be near it. There was something forbidden about this coat and I had to figure out what it could be.

The coat lived in the front hall closet. Kids coats and casual adult coats lived in the back hall closet with the shoes and boots and mittens and hats but the good coats lived in the front hall closet. I don't remember what else was in the closet but my dad's work coats, their raincoats, the coats my mom wore out to dinner, all neatly hung in the closet under the front hall staircase.

We Know

Since I was "not allowed" to wear or play with or even touch the rabbit fur coat unless my mom was there, of course that is what I wanted to do. But I also knew that I could not make any noise or move around with the coat because that would attract attention. Our living room was the farthest room from the kitchen so it provided a bit of privacy. Though I was not to play in the living room, I was allowed to read or listen to music in the living room—that is where the record player was. And the kitchen was where my mom was most late afternoons as she prepared dinner. And I would be told to amuse myself during this time either doing homework, or reading or playing by myself as my mother would have her hands full between making dinner and watching my younger sister. So I would put on a stack of records (45's being my favorite and my all-time favorite song at the time was The Purple People Eater; I have no idea why but I thought it was hilarious) in the living room and then I would go and sit in the closet with the door ajar and snuggle up with the coat, which reached all the way to the floor, while listening to music. I got away with this charade a number of times.

The inside of the coat had some sort of satin lining, so it was not fun to actually be inside the coat. I would sit beside the coat and wrap it around me so that I could feel the fur. But then I got to thinking about the rabbits. And the fact that rabbits were small. And the coat was big. And the fact that I had a rabbit, named Bunny, when we lived in Cincinnati. When we moved to Michigan, I was not allowed to bring Bunny with me.

THE RABBITS

I don't remember clearly how we got Bunny but I think I won her at a church festival when I was six and we moved when I was seven. My mom found a farm for Bunny and we took her to the farm where I was told she would live a happy life. I was told she "belonged" on a farm. The farm had goats and chickens too. I don't remember much about it other than the fact that I had to leave my rabbit but my mom's cat was moving with us. It did not seem fair to me. I cried the whole time we were at the farm. Now I wonder what did happen to that poor rabbit.

And I would think about Jill, the German Shepherd I loved and our calico cat, Maxine, and how their hair fell out and did not stay together. So how did they make a coat from rabbit fur? I could not figure it out. I also don't remember ever comparing the rabbit "fur" to my own "hair."

I saw humans as being fundamentally different from animals even, already, at eight years old.

I finally asked my mother, on a day when she wore the coat and they were going to some fancy dinner. I remember she put me off, saying something like, "They make it from rabbits."

And I said, "But how? I don't know how."

And she said, "They just do. Don't worry about it." And I knew then that they killed the rabbits. I don't know how I knew, but I remember feeling sick to my stomach. She only lied to me when it was something bad. Something she thought was too old for me to know. I knew her tone and the look on her face when she did not want me to know something. It only happened occasionally and this was one of those times.

I never got caught hanging out with the rabbit coat—one of the few things I got away with. Or at least I don't remember getting caught. And I never hung out with the rabbit coat after I learned that the rabbits actually died for that stupid coat. I came to hate the coat and dreaded when my mother wore it as she wanted to be noticed for it. Attention-seeking was not her way so that was odd in and of itself.

I have no idea what happened to the coat. That was in the late 1960's. I don't ever remember seeing it once I had moved out of the house as an adult. Eventually my parents moved to Florida so their need for winter gear reduced dramatically. But I also don't remember any conversation about the coat or its fate.

THE RABBITS

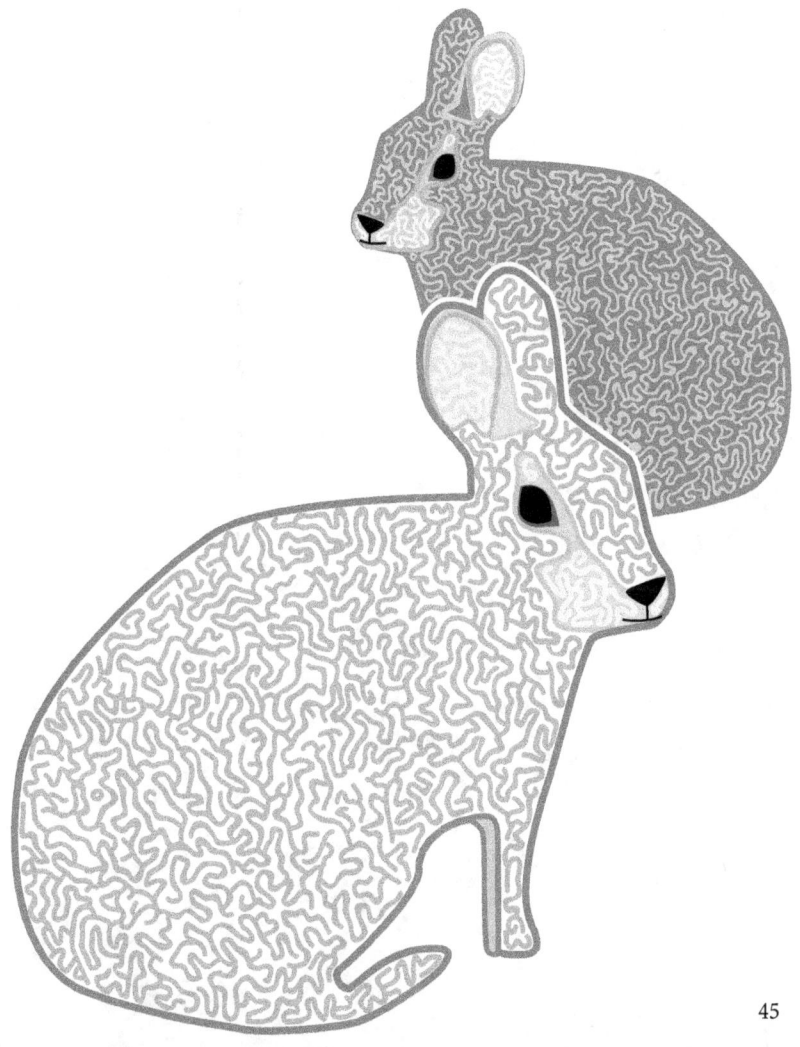

*Chickens are proud
and inquisitive
and live in large,
stable social groups.*

*They feel joy and fear
and are very curious.*

*Chickens are good mothers
whose wings
protect their babies.*

*I knew when I was twelve
and no on had to tell me*

*that killing and cooking
the chickens from next door*

*— the very individuals
who came through the fence
to play with my horse —*

was wrong.

The Chickens

When I was twelve, my parents agreed to buy me my own horse. I was spending so much time with Flint and I didn't really have many friends. I was one of the weird kids in school. We lived in a small town, Northville, Michigan. At the time it was an actual small town, now it is just part of the contiguous suburbs of Detroit. It's about 30 miles Northwest of downtown Detroit, mostly West, a little North. We were Catholic and there was one Catholic Church, Our Lady of Victory, and an attached school serving grades 1-8. Though it wasn't a one room school, it was one room for each grade—so literally eight classrooms in the whole school. The church was attached to the school via a covered porch. I attended Our Lady of Victory from 3rd through 8th grade.

I always considered myself one of the weird kids because I didn't fit any of the labels easily. I was a really good student without trying. I loved to read and I read a lot, often getting into trouble at home for reading "above my age," whatever that actually meant. I memorized well and tested well. But I also questioned authority all the time. I pointed out things that were unfair, in my eyes at least, about me or about other kids. I got bullied (due to my good grades, poor athletic ability, glasses and braces) and I stood up to kids who bullied other kids. I learned sign language with another student in 3rd grade and got in loads of trouble because Mrs. Johnson didn't like us "talking" during class.

Eventually we were not allowed to sign at all. And she is the one who read Helen Kellers' story to us, so that punishment seemed especially unfair. And the fact that we were learning a second language did not seem to occur to any of the adults. Nor did they consider that we might find employment as a sign language interpreter in the future. It still seems so short-sighted and one of the many problems with our current education system. And no, I never did learn American Sign Language (ASL), and yes, I have always regretted that.

And I hated milk. And all children are automatically assumed to love milk. At the public school I could get away with not drinking it because the school was much bigger and there was an actual cafeteria. At Our Lady of Victory, we brought our lunch from home and ate at our desks each day and a couple of the kids in the class would have "milk duty" where they went to get the milk from the refrigerators in the basement of the church and bring the correct number of cartons into the classroom. We each paid five cents a carton for the milk and you had to have special arrangements to get chocolate milk. I didn't like either

THE CHICKENS

flavor (though I would drink the chocolate from time to time but my mother would not give me permission for chocolate milk) and would totally refuse to drink the "white milk" and then I would get written up for disobeying every day. Sometimes someone else would drink it for me, but not often enough to count.

We moved to Northville from Cincinnati in June 1967, the summer between first and second grade for me. Our Lady of Victory did not have room for me in the second grade so I had to attend the public school for one year. This was a big change for my family, as the Catholic community in Cincinnati was much bigger and more robust. Just about all of my parents' social life revolved around the church there, and all the kids attended Catholic schools. It's just the way it was done. In Northville, we could get on the waiting list for the Catholic grade school, but my older sister (entering her senior year in high school) and my older brother (entering his freshman year) both attended the public school, Northville High—home of the Mustangs, the only thing I really liked about it. The Catholic High Schools were closer to Detroit and there were no buses, so my parents sent all of us to Northville High, a public school. I tried hard to get them to send me to the public junior high but they would not agree.

So, as I ended 7th grade, in the too-small Catholic school where I could not hide or fade into the background because the place was just too small, I started getting into trouble. I hung out with a few other girls who were also good students but who didn't like the confinement of the small Catholic school. We wore makeup to school. We wore shorts under our uniforms so that we could do somersaults and run around more easily. We left school grounds during lunch hours and smoked cigarettes. We refused to answer questions. We were mild miscreants. My older sister had been in a lot of trouble as a teenager and my parents wanted to avoid that with me so agreeing to buy me a horse was both a bribe and a threat. A bribe to "be good" and a threat that the horse could be taken away if I was "bad."

Our next door neighbors to the East raised chickens, I thought for eggs. Sometimes we got eggs from them but not very often. We did not know these people well; I can't even remember their names and our houses were not visible to each other. There was a small wooded area between our house and theirs and they did not have kids my age so I didn't pay much attention to them. Our house sat on three acres of land and was basically square. I don't know how much land they owned, but their property was a long rectangle.

We fenced in about a ½ acre at the back of our yard that took advantage of chain link fences on the South and East of our yard. We added a wooden fence on the West and South sides to make a small pasture. The East end of the pasture used the chain link fence that also kept the chickens in their coop and pen. As soon as Lady Ebony moved into the pasture, chickens from next door would come over to spend time with her. They were always finding ways through the fence, or making ways through the fence to hang out. They seemed to like each other a lot. It was always up to me to pick up the chicken and take her

THE CHICKENS

back to the neighbors. The chickens were always calm and quiet. They never fought being picked up and I always thought they were very cool.

One day I was coming home from school when I saw my mother walking from the neighbor's house to our house with a package under her arm. It was a paper bag with something inside. I was walking across the yard from the West side street where the bus dropped me off and she was walking from the East. As we met near the back porch, I asked her what she had. It was an innocent question.

My mother smiled in a weird way and said, "Dinner."

Confused, I asked, "What?"

When we entered the kitchen, she put the package on the counter and took something wrapped in butcher paper out.

I stared at it and exclaimed something like, "Are you kidding?! Is that a chicken from next door? How could you?!"

And she nastily said, "Oh, stop it. I've been buying chickens from them for months and you never knew and you ate them with no problem. It's no big deal. They're no different than the chickens at the grocery store."

But for me there was a big difference between the chicken (which seemed like "meat" and unrelated to living beings) we bought at the store and the chickens (living, breathing, friends to my horse, gentle creatures in my arms) from next door. It's hard to admit I thought this way. I remember feeling sick to my stomach when she told me. And I remember feeling different from my mother and other people in general. Why did this not bother her? Why did it bother me so viscerally? I felt so guilty—I had carried chickens to their deaths. I could have saved them. I could have refused to take them back. I had been eating chickens from next door for months without knowing that I knew them. Eating someone I knew seemed cannibalistic. Knowing that my mother hid the truth from me seemed like such a betrayal. Again I felt alone, as if no one else shared this thinking with me.

I made such a scene with my mother that she put that chicken in the freezer and we ate something else that night. I don't remember what. It was probably another "meat" and somehow I did not see it as another formerly living being. I have no idea why I did not make the connection then. I did stop eating chicken, at least at home. I remember as a young adult eating chicken at events when it was served, but I don't remember buying it.

My mother stopped buying chickens from next door. She would go grocery shopping and show me the package with the chicken inside. But I had seen the chicken as a warm, loving, living being and I could not unsee it. Chicken would end up on my plate, but I would push it around rather than eat it.

And I did stop taking chickens back. If they came through the fence I let them be and refused to take them back.

I don't know if the neighbors came to get them or if the chickens got themselves back through the fence. I suspect they fortified the fence so that the chickens couldn't get through because I don't remember many chickens in the pasture after that event.

THE CHICKENS

Cows are gentle giants,
contemplative, collaborative,
and compassionate.

They form lifelong friendships,
enjoy intellectual challenges,
and jump for joy
when they solve a problem.

I knew when I was sixteen
and no had to tell me

that making friends with a calf
— playing with her,
caring for her,
bathing and grooming her
for the 4-H show —
only to kill her,
dismember her,
and eat her

was wrong.

The Cow

I don't remember how Danielle and I met. I think it was at school though I don't have a specific memory of our meeting. I liked her name. And I liked that she lived outside of town, on a small farm. She was kind of a tom-boy and I fancied myself a bit of a tom-boy too. I loved horses and was comfortable around them, and her family had a small farm and I thought this formed a connection for us. They grew some vegetables and sold them at a farmstand in front of their house. Danielle hated working there during the summer but she was the labor pool and she was expected to be there.

They also raised animals and had chickens, pigs, and a few cows. This was not a big operation and definitely not a factory farm. The animals spent most of their time outside and ate real food. As far as I remember, Danielle's dad did almost all the work with help from her mom, Danielle, and her little brother. They might have hired some help at certain times of the year but I did not see anyone else there. Danielle did not like being at her house so we didn't go there. I had the impression she didn't like the fact that they farmed. Mostly we hung out after school at the new Burger Chef —a big deal at the time—or occasionally at the library or at my house. But I wanted to go to Danielle's house because I was curious. So one day my mom drove me over after school. I don't remember how the invitation happened, but we ended up there one day.

So Danielle and I were friends, but we never became "best" friends, as our lives were quite different and we spent some time together but not a lot. I think we both thought of ourselves as outsiders but for different reasons and that was a point of connection for us.

Our town was small and was actually a suburb of Detroit. It was a distinct, small town at the time and Detroit seemed far away, but it was not rural and very few people had farm animals. There were some horses. But no one else I knew had farm animals other than the chickens next door.

I remember the day I was at Danielle's house and learned about Daisy. It was a surprise to learn that Danielle was involved with 4-H and was raising a cow during my junior year in high school, her senior year.

The cow's name was Daisy and she was treated differently than the other cows. She was allowed in the barn much of the time. Danielle groomed her, bathed her, got her used to a halter and a lead (a totally different prospect with a cow than a horse I was to learn) and spent a little bit of time with her most days. I was really excited to meet her. I believe it was March, and the day was a bit warm and sunny and it was a decent day to be outside.

Danielle did not want to take me to the barn to meet Daisy. I remember we were listening to Crosby, Stills and Nash and looking out her window and could see the barn but could not see Daisy inside. We were in the bedroom and I guess Danielle's mom heard us and came to the door and encouraged her to take me out and show me Daisy. Her mom sounded proud of Danielle. Danielle seemed ashamed, making me confused. But out to the barn we went.

When we got to the barn, Daisy was in one of the stalls eating hay. We walked up to the door and Daisy walked over and put her head out wanting to be petted, just like a horse would. I immediately put my hand on her forehead and started rubbing. I was impressed with the difference between horses and cows. Daisy seemed so much sturdier to me—wider and stronger, even though she was young. She clearly liked to have her forehead rubbed.

But Danielle pulled me away and said not to give her too much attention. When I asked why not, Danielle told me that she would go to slaughter as soon as the 4-H show was over and her meat would be put in the freezer to be eaten the following year. We shouldn't make her feel like a pet, because she wasn't.

I was shocked. I felt like I had been punched. I don't know what I was expecting but I could not believe that someone could raise an animal from infancy (Daisy was born to a cow that Danielle's father owned), feed her, groom her, teach her to take a halter and lead and gain her trust just to kill her and eat her. I felt like throwing up as we stood there, in front of Daisy, having this conversation.

This was very confusing to me. I liked Danielle. She was not a monster. But this felt like a monstrous thing to me. When I found my voice I asked her how she could do this—take part in this treachery, though I did not say that part out loud. And Danielle told me this is the way the world works. We have to eat. We eat cows. It's as simple as that. Then she walked out of the barn and back to the house.

I lost the connection I thought Danielle and I shared in that moment. Now I wonder about Danielle's reluctance to share her home with me and her callousness about Daisy. I wonder if (or imagine that) she was simply protecting herself the best she could. I could leave and go home where we at least said we loved the cat and dog and horse even while we ate the chicken and pig and cow. But Danielle had no place to go, no one to turn to, no way to hide the ugliness.

And I never did meet the pigs at her house because they were pigs, and Danielle and her mom thought the pigs were dirty and nasty and not worthy of interaction. These were farm animals and animals were how her dad made money so they were not ever seen as pets to be played with. Even the dog lived outside and was used to help control the other animals; he was not a beloved member of the family.

This philosophy was new to me. Though my family ate meat, dairy and eggs, we also treated pets as family members.

Or at least as worthy of respect and care. I did not recognize the hypocrisy at the time.

We never talked about Daisy or 4-H again. I never went back to her house. I don't remember ever being invited to her house again either. We remained friendly but not really friends. I felt like I was missing something, not understanding something about all this, about Danielle. But it wasn't Danielle that I was missing something about. It was me. It was our society. I continued to eat cows after this. Somehow, I could not imagine eating a cow I knew, I could not imagine sending a cow I knew to slaughter. But I didn't even think about eating the cow parts that came from the grocery store or were in those burgers at Burger Chef. I also never talked to anyone else about this experience. I think I knew that most people would not understand my revulsion and I did not want to have to defend myself. I did not know anything about 4-H at the time but have come to see 4-H as one of the most effective ways we indoctrinate children into normalizing violence and perpetuating speciesism.

On Being a Mirror

Sometimes I think that being an early adopter of an ethical vegan lifestyle means that we become mirrors for our friends and family members. Humans (pretty much all of us, the vast majority of the time) like to have our decisions supported or ignored. We don't like having our current or even past behavior held up in any way that could be considered negative. Calling our decisions in to question, holding our choices up to the light of common sense—or scientific fact—is often very uncomfortable for us. Much of this book does just that—sometimes implicitly, sometimes explicitly.

I am unaware of how change can possibly happen without personal discomfort. We have to see and believe that something was not right so that we can change our behavior to make it right with what we know now.

Maya Angelou said: "Do the best you can until you know better. Then when you know better, do better." So we can all believe that we are doing the best we can do with what we know. And by paying attention to the mirrors that we find in other people, we can get more information so that we can know better and then do better.

*Pigs are smart enough
to play video games
against chimpanzees
and win.*

*Pigs are peaceful,
rarely show anger
and are very kind
to each other.*

*I knew when I was twenty
and no one had to tell me*

*that "celebrating"
with co-workers
while a teenage pig with
an apple wedged in his mouth
roasted over an open fire
to please our palates*

was wrong.

The Pig

It's funny—I seem to be an extrovert, sure of myself and confident around people. I have strong opinions and I am not shy to say them out loud. But I'm not confident or sure of myself in so many ways. I much prefer to be in the background. I like to sit in the back of the room, near an exit, so that I can watch what is happening without being watched and so that I can leave if I need to. I don't want the spotlight to be on me.

I married when I was twenty. I believe this was my "get out of the house" marriage. It was so much easier to be on my own with a husband than to be on my own with just myself. He was a nice guy and I hope he has done well in life though I have not kept up with him at all. His parents did not like me. Their dream for him was that he would become a doctor but his dream was that he would get an MBA from Michigan and work in computer programming. He announced this decision after meeting me and in their eyes, I was the cause of his decision. I was not. He was working on his bachelors in biochemistry from Michigan when we met and he hated it. He did not want to work in the medical field in any capacity. Their blame never made sense but it was real and damaging to us. And it now helps me to understand why people blame others when the world does not work out the way they want it to. It cannot be their own "fault" or simply fate, it must have been caused by someone else with bad intent.

We married in May 1980 after he graduated with that MBA and I was entering my junior year of college, majoring in Social Work (just more evidence that I was not right for him though I never understood that logic either). We moved to Midland, Michigan, where he took a job with Dow Chemical Company. That very first summer, there was a company cookout that we were invited to, expected to attend, really. I did not want to go. We knew very few people. I was only twenty and most of the people were middle aged or older. I was quite progressive and most people in town were quite conservative. I was studying Social Work and wanted to help marginalized people while these people were chemists, engineers, biologists and many people already had MBAs or PhDs. It was quite intimidating to think about, much less to actually attend.

Our presence was expected and we were going. It was on a Saturday, at a local park in July. There were a lot of people in attendance. We had only been in town since the first of June and did not know much about the area. I would not start school until September and I had not yet found a job. The picnic was of course casual, so everyone was in shorts and t-shirts, kids were running around everywhere, there was plenty of alcohol.

THE PIG

The tables were long and set up under a very large tent. The food was served buffet style and everyone contributed a dish to share while the main dish and the alcohol was provided by the company.

Midland was the quintessential company town. It makes me so uncomfortable now and it seemed odd to me even then. Dow Chemical was started there in 1890 and Midland boasts many things—the highest per capita rate of Phds in the country (at least that was what they claimed in 1980), a high standard of living, a high per capita income, a great public school system. Dow made all those things happen of course and the people appreciated it by naming a bunch of things in town after the family: Dow Gardens, Dow High School, the Chemics was the name of the Midland High football team, Chemical Bank; I'm sure you get the idea.

But then the town started naming everything "Midland" so as not to become too much of a company town, so there is the Midland Center for the Arts, Midland Tennis Center, Midland Community Center—all supported extensively by Dow and its suppliers. And these are all great and reasonably priced and accessible amenities. On paper this all seems so grand. Yet the reality is something a bit darker—the question to newcomers in town is "what division do you work for?" not "what do you do?" And for those who don't work for the company, there really is a sense that you work for the support of the company and its employees; you are a second rate citizen. And Dow Chemical means so much to the community (in a large sense, Dow *is* the community) that no one questions anything Dow does. And when we are talking about large quantities of chemicals, there could, maybe, theoretically, be some problems. Dow-Corning corporation also has its headquarters in Midland.

Diversity is not really a thing in Midland. Or at least it wasn't then. Just a quick side story—in 1989, I was divorced and bought a small, two bedroom, two bath house and quickly found that owning a house was a bit more expensive than anticipated. I took in a renter who was attending Northwood University, a private automotive university in town. Alfred was from Charlotte, North Carolina. We met over the phone when I answered an ad he placed in our local paper. We had several phone calls to determine if we could share a house. I was 30, Alfred was 26. He was coming out of the Navy and his plan was to own car dealerships in North Carolina and Northwood was a great place to get such an education.

On the third call, Alfred said "I think you should know I'm Black and I want to make sure that won't be a problem for you."

Honestly, I had deduced he was Black based on his voice. I assumed he believed I was white based on my voice and where I lived. I was not prepared for this announcement and was not sure what to say in response so I modified his statement back to him: "Oh, well, I think you should know I'm white and I want to make sure that won't be a problem for you." There was a moment of silence and Alfred burst out laughing. I joined him and we decided we could share a house. And he was the best renter I could imagine. Though that's another whole story.

Back to the issue of diversity in Midland. After Alfred moved in and started school, he came home one day and told me that he had wandered around Main Street, going into many of the stores to see what they sold.

He felt increasingly uncomfortable when no one engaged with him in any of the stores and he finally went into the posh men's store and asked, "Where are all the Black people?"

And they told him they were all in Saginaw.

He didn't know that Saginaw was the next city to the south of Midland and was home to several auto factories and had a large Black population. At that time there were literally almost no Black people living in Midland.

So the picnic was very white, with a couple of very smart brown people, from India or Asia, who were doing their time at world headquarters. It was a very homogeneous group of book-smart people working on making "better living through chemistry" a reality (and yes, that really was, maybe still is, Dow's tagline). I was already feeling intimidated because I was young, new to town, new to marriage, much more interested in social justice issues than chemicals, working on a social work degree, trying to project myself as a feminist in a very masculine space without actually pissing anyone off or offending my husband's colleagues or boss and an animal lover underpinning it all. I did not feel a strong sense of belonging when we got to the park.

I knew the event was called a pig roast. I had no idea they were actually roasting an entire pig. I had never heard of such a thing before, much less been to one. As we left our car and walked toward the tent, one of my husband's colleagues met us and introduced his wife to us. They were about ten years older than us and had three kids so we didn't have a lot in common but they were very nice. I was still carrying the potato salad we brought and she offered to take it and put it on the table. He took us to the drinks area where I chose a diet coke. I wasn't twenty-one yet and didn't want to push the issue. We chatted a bit and watched the kids play and met a few more people. It was a bit overwhelming to me and I knew I wouldn't remember many names. I was just focusing on being pleasant and not doing anything wrong in a situation I could not relate to.

The announcement was made that people could begin filling their plates and we got in line for the buffet. As we got closer I noticed that the food tables were lined up on the edges of the tent in a U-shape, with people lining up on each side of the tables. We proceeded through the long side of the U, on the outside of the tent, filling our plates with salads and side dishes. As we turned the corner, we could see the end of the smaller table and the main event.

There was a whole pig, with a rod through his body, his skin blistered and splitting, his eyes looking straight at me and an apple obscenely wedged in his mouth. I gasped and stopped still. I felt like I could not breathe. My heart pounded. I ate bacon and pork chops. I knew they came from pigs. But I had never seen a whole pig, with head and legs and tail and ears stuck on a piece of metal, being carved up to eat. It was horrific. And the apple, the apple got to me the most. It was not cooked. It was still firm and red. Someone had wedged it in the pigs' mouth after he had been roasted. It seemed so barbaric. It was such a surreal feeling. I heard people talking and laughing. I saw children running around playing. I watched people filling their paper plates with salads and sides and eagerly taking the pieces of the pig they were offered, oohing and ahhing over the smells. And everyone acted as though this was perfectly normal. I wanted to scream and run away.

But of course I did not. My husband saw my reaction and nudged me forward with a plea in his eyes to not make a scene. I filled my plate with the next veggie dish on the table and announced that my plate was full, I would have to come back for seconds later and I left the line. We had not chosen seats beforehand so I stood to the side while he finished getting his food and we joined some colleagues at a long table in the middle of the tent. No one seemed to notice that I did not have pig on my plate. I sat for a bit without eating or talking and just let the whole scene wash around me. I finally found the ability to eat a bit and finished the event without embarrassing him or myself though he heard the next Monday that many people found me shy. I wasn't shy. I just didn't feel like I belonged in that group, in that setting.

My understanding of what we do to animals fundamentally changed that day. I did not recognize it at the time, but that picnic, that bizarre display of overt human aggression toward animals, would have a significant impact on me, but not for more than a decade.

Amazingly, I did not stop eating animals at that moment. I did not even stop eating pigs. Though I think I stopped eating them for a while. We were not big into eating pork anyway. But I began clearly moving away from eating meat, often choosing dishes to order or cook that used little meat or none at all. I'm sorry to say that I did continue or maybe even increased eating dairy and eggs; mac and cheese, veggie lasagnas, burritos and enchiladas, grilled cheese sandwiches, veggie soups all became common fare. I loved large salads and never included meat, and rarely added cheese though I loved dairy-based dressings. I also became a breakfast-for-lunch (or dinner) fan, having pancakes or french toast or eggs and hashbrowns for any meal at a restaurant that served them at those times. All to stay away from eating flesh without actually taking a stand as a vegetarian. I don't think I believed it was really an option, to stop eating meat all together at that time.

THE PIG

*Deer are highly social beings
with women living communally,
caring for their infants and children.*

*Groups of teenage boys hang out together,
finding food and staying safe.*

The men are territorial and live a more solitary life.

*I knew when I was thirty two
and no one had to tell me*

*that stalking, baiting
and shooting unarmed deer
for fun*

was wrong.

> *But someone did have to point out —
> even though I disapproved of hunting,
> finding it cruel and unnecessary,
> every individual deer had a chance
> to outrun the arrow or the bullet*
>
> *while not a single cow or pig or chicken
> ever had a chance against the slaughterhouse blade.*

The Deer

I vividly remember the evening I gave up eating meat. It was November 14, 1992, a Saturday. I was living with Reko, a relationship that was becoming more strained all the time.

We had been together since 1989, living together since 1991. The living together had seemed like a good idea at the beginning but not so much by then. I think I knew it was over even then, but did not know how to extricate myself. Things were complicated in that I had left my well-paying, high(ish) status job with great benefits and a future path to be the director of a small, idealistic housing organization, and I was making very little money and the only benefit was health insurance. That's another story...

One thing about Reko I did like was that he was a really good cook. He had taught himself to cook as he wanted great food but did not always want to go out to eat. He listened to a radio cooking show most days and often tried those recipes, often from memory. Or he would write in to the show for the recipe to be mailed to him—in the days before the internet. And he shopped and cooked in the "European tradition," at least that's how he described it to me.

Reko owned a fireplace installation company and mostly worked as a subcontractor to builders, installing fireplaces in new housing. He had one employee, so he did installations as well as all the other activities of business ownership. There was no office or store but he did have a small warehouse, really a large garage, that he rented as a place to keep building supplies and his trailer.

He left early for work, generally about 7:00am, and was usually home no later than 3:30pm. He would then shower, do paperwork, and then decide what to make for dinner and run to the grocery store and buy food for that night's dinner and anything else he might need, like paper or cleaning products. There was no weekly meal planning or grocery shopping. I thought it slightly strange, but he said he never knew what he might be in the mood for until the last minute. There was a grocery store about five minutes from the house so it was no big deal to shop everyday.

Looking back, I am a bit embarrassed, but the first meal he cooked for me in the fall of 1989 was a tossed salad with balsamic vinaigrette, filet mignon with mushrooms, garlic and shallots and fettuccine alfredo. Dessert was fresh strawberries dipped in chocolate. Very little nutritional value and of course a ton of fat. I think this is the very definition of a heart attack on a plate. There was a fine red wine to accompany it all.

Fast forward to Saturday, November 14, 1992. I was leaving

for a week in Wisconsin on Sunday, November 15 with a number of my colleagues. We were partnering with a group in Wisconsin to bring the ideas of Person Centered Planning across the state.

We were visiting multiple cities and holding day-long workshops Monday through Thursday and driving home on Friday. There were seven or eight of us on the trip. We rented a van so that we could all ride together with all our stuff. It was going to be fun, productive and meaningful. We were still on a work high from all we had done the previous years. It was a fabulous feeling. So I was feeling pretty good about the upcoming week. The stress of my living situation was at the back of my mind. I remember the weather was not horrible, and we grilled burgers out on the back patio even though it was November. Reko would make burgers with quality beef and add spices to the mix so his burgers were always special, at least according to him.

I was never much of a meat eater and required all of my meat to be very well done, a situation that annoyed him (and chefs at any decent restaurant) to no end. But I would not eat meat that had any pinkness or blood in evidence.

Anyway, the burgers were served with homemade beer battered, fried onion rings (health was not much of a concern at that time), and the usual onions, tomatoes and lettuce. Dinner was almost always about 7:30 or 8:00pm. After dinner, we watched some TV, ending with the news.

Deer hunting was always a big deal in Michigan. Bow season started in October and went through December, but gun season was November 15 - 30 every year. It seemed like huge numbers of men (I'm sure there were a few women but they were never talked about and I did not know any) took their vacations and had big traditions around gun season each year.

I had worked for a number of years managing group homes for people with disabilities all over central and northern Michigan. For several years, my territory included Lansing to the south and Traverse City to the north, with several group homes in between. I was on the road a lot. These were the days before cell phones. I was single and lived alone. At that time I lived in Midland and Traverse City was a two-and-a-half or three hour drive depending on which route I took and road conditions. It was a beautiful drive no matter the route and passed many, many acres of forest land.

So during gun season I often saw dead deer bodies laying on the side of the roads missing their heads. It seems that many hunters just wanted the head of the deer as a trophy and left the body to rot or for other animals to eat. I never understood and still don't understand mounting those heads in houses, offices or restaurants. What is that all about? We are, rightfully, understandably, thoroughly repulsed at the idea (not the reality) of keeping a dead human body part around but we mount animal heads on our walls and think that is cool? I don't get it.

One time I remember driving home from Traverse City to Midland, leaving about 6pm in the dark. Soon after leaving Traverse City, the road took a left sweeping turn, downhill and I saw a pickup truck on the side of the road in the distance with a light shining into the woods. As I got closer I saw three men in the bed of the pickup with rifles. I pulled over a small distance behind them to figure out what was going on. They had a salt block and a bunch of carrots on the ground just outside the woods and they were apparently waiting for deer to come to the bait. This was illegal, even in Michigan, even that long ago.

I sat in my car trying to decide what to do. I actually opened my car door and put one foot out onto the pavement when the thought occurred to me that there were three men in that truck, with guns, blatantly engaging in illegal activity. Probably drinking alcohol as well. And I was going to... do what, exactly? Ask them nicely to go away? Did I mention this was before cell phones? And that I was single and lived alone. And no one would know I was missing until the next day when I didn't show up for work.

So my imagination ran away with me, but I still decided it was not a good idea to intervene. I put my foot back in the car, closed my door and drove on. Right past them with my heart pounding fast and they laughed at me. I think I made the right decision. I did stop at the next phone booth I found, about 45 minutes later and reported them to the police. I am quite certain nothing came of it.

So on that Saturday evening as we watched the ten o'clock news, the news anchor gleefully announced that gun season started the next morning and the weather guy talked about how the weather would impact hunting for the coming week and everything seemed focused on killing innocent animals who just wanted to live their lives. I reacted and shared how much I hated hunting and recounted my stories of seeing headless dead deer on the side of the road and I became pretty upset and judgmental. Then Reko looked at me and said, "How hypocritical. You just happily ate a hamburger."

I sputtered something, I think. I remember being confused and angry. Then deeply embarrassed and ashamed when he said something like, "That cow you ate never had a chance, but every single deer has a chance to run. What difference do you possibly see?"

That was one of the most profound conversations of my life. Even though it was very short. It did not have the impact Reko imagined. He simply thought I should not be judgmental about hunting and hunters. He had no problem eating meat, fish, eggs, dairy; he was actually quite the adventurous eater. We went to sleep without having much more conversation but my mind was working overtime. How could I continue eating some animals while advocating for others? How did that make any sense? I remember lying in bed that night thinking and realizing that I had to change.

Fortunately I was away from Reko and my usual routine for the next six days. I announced to my colleagues that I was not eating meat in protest of gun season. I would not eat any flesh between November 15 - 30. They all scoffed at me and told me how hard it would be to eat while we were on the road. It was not, of course. Though I think I ate a lot of cheese while in Wisconsin. I am ashamed to admit that I did not understand the realities of the dairy or egg industries for a very long time.

As the days went on and I found that meat free meals were easy to find or customize, I came to really like living another value, acting on principle. I was doing work that emancipated people with disabilities from the confines of group homes and institutions and that our culture had basically thrown away or simply ignored. Now I added a personal action that upheld life in a new way, a way that I could see and feel and taste three times a day. Vegetarianism was still quite weird in 1992. And it felt good to be on that edge.

I never returned to eating meat.

We Know

"That cow you ate never had a chance,

but every single deer has a chance to run.

What difference do you possibly see?"

THE DEER

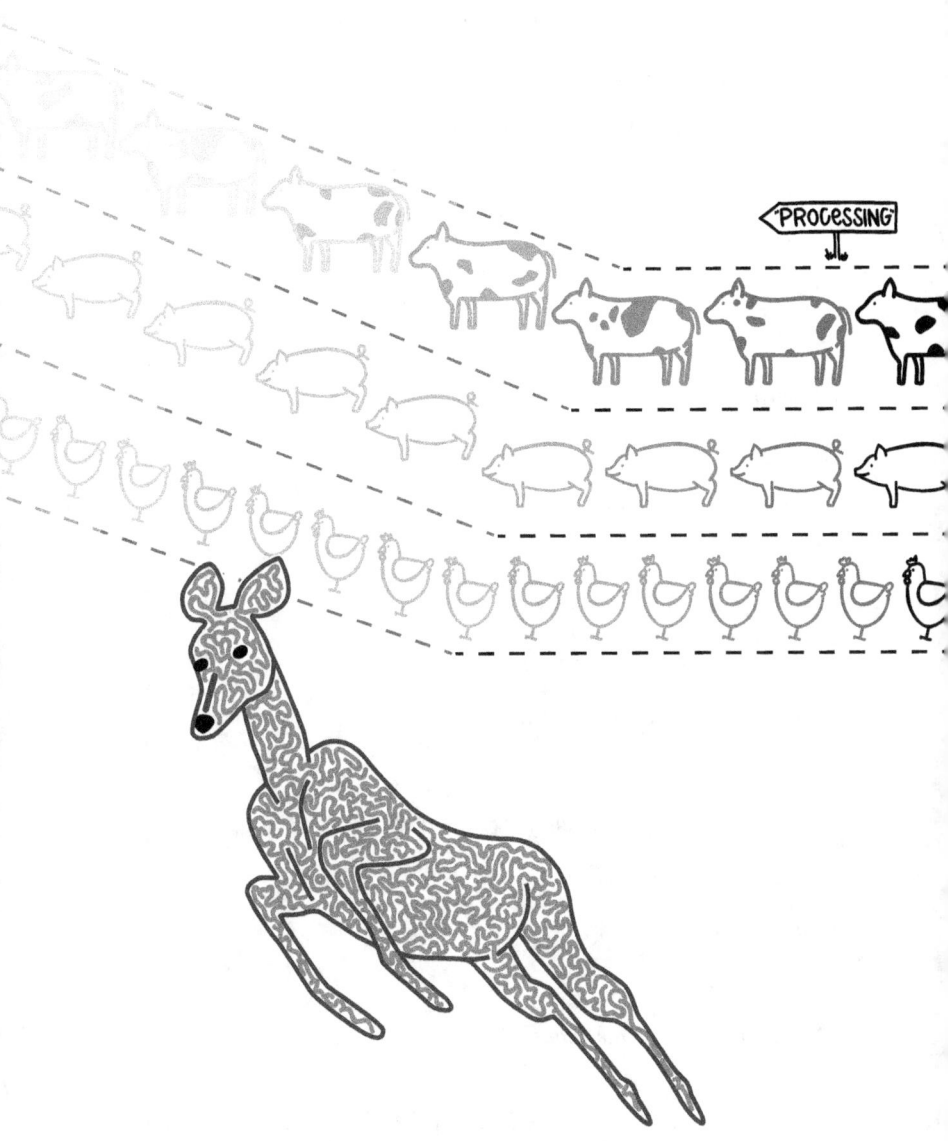

I knew when I was five and no one had to tell me.
I knew when I was eight and no one had to tell me.
I knew when I was twelve and no one had to tell me.
I knew when I was sixteen and no one had to tell me.
I knew when I was twenty and no one had to tell me.
I knew when I was thirty-two. And yet...

the confinement
the torture
the killing
the eating

of sentient beings continues

> *with numbers so large*
> *they are incomprehensible -*
> *70 BILLION a year worldwide.*

More animals die for human food each week
than all the humans killed in all the wars
in all of recorded history.

When will we all know enough to stop?

> *And when will the adults support the children*
> *who already know?*

The Invitation

I often wonder what might have happened had I been supported by the adults in my life to explore my feelings, delve into the questions I had, look at the truth as I discovered it. What might have changed about my life? What might have changed about my family? Would I have had the same career? The same level of self-confidence? It's an interesting thought experiment. Supporting your child's thinking, taking your child seriously, will undoubtedly result in a child and then an adult who is curious, thoughtful and self-confident.

I chose to write the stories behind the poem that is illustrated in the children's book *I Knew When I Was Five*, to help adults think about these conversations they will have with their children from the child's perspective. Our culture does a

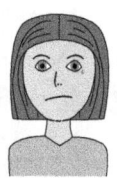

near universal job of expecting animal eating from our children. We do not question eating animals. At least not those our culture deems "food animals." Which animals (and their parts and secretions) are eaten varies by culture and even within cultures, but most cultures simply take eating animals as the norm, the expectation, the thing we do and have always done. People, including parents, do not question the validity of these cultural norms.

When children balk at eating animals, and it turns out that many do as toddlers and preschoolers, (with more joining this group as they get older) the advice parents are given is about how to get children to eat animals, not about whether or not eating animals is good for our health, ethically correct or environmentally sound.

I searched and searched for articles or studies about supporting children to not eat animals and I could find very few. (Animal Rights organizations have many helpful resources but those are not the resources that come up when one searches with the words "Help—my child won't eat meat!" or something similar). There could be some that I did not find, but I do know that information about how to get children to eat animals is much easier to find. And most of the information that is written takes a humorous view of children refusing to eat animals rather than asking parents to see this as a serious concern to be explored.

Here are some of the easy-to-find articles about toddlers who don't want to eat meat:

- *Toddler Won't Eat Meat? Read This* from

Yummy Toddler Food [14]

- *5 Things To Do When Your Toddler Won't Eat Meat* from Find Your Mom Tribe [15]
- *4 Tips From A Dietitian To Get Your Child To Eat Meat* from First Step Nutrition [16]

Most of the articles do include information on the need for protein in children (not nearly as much as we tend to believe) and plant-based foods that contain protein (though the articles tend to focus on dairy and eggs first and some include beans and nuts). But almost none of the articles address the issue of ethics. They talk about children being "accidental vegetarians." What is *accidental* about a child proclaiming they don't want to eat animals?

Most parents take a toddler's or young child's resistance to eating meat as "a phase" or the child being a "picky eater" and spend no time considering the ethics of eating animals or seriously consider the validity of supporting their child to not eat animals. The truth appears to be very different. Children have their own thoughts about what they want to eat and it's possible that many of their parents aren't listening closely enough. Consider the BBC Good Food's survey of children's eating habits from the summer of 2021. The survey asked 1,000 children, ages 5-16 about their eating habits and how they would like to eat. According to the BBC's results:

> "8% of children are following a vegan diet and of those who don't follow a vegan diet, 15% would like to. They also found that 13%

of children are vegetarian and around one in five (21%) of children who are not currently vegetarian would like to be." [17]

This means that a total of 57% of the children surveyed do not want to eat meat: 23% are or want to eat vegan, and 34% are or want to be vegetarian. Fifty-seven percent! Obviously children are aware of the cruelty, sustainability and health issues inherent in eating a meat-based diet. The survey did not go further into these details (but did ask about cooking skills) and I find it curious that so little is studied about what children want to eat and why. The literature is overwhelmingly focused on how to get children to eat meat, not how to support children to eat a healthy plant based diet while simultaneously following their compassionate, empathic desires.

We are selling our children short and impacting their future on this fragile planet with our inattentiveness.

All parents want their children to be happy, healthy and successful, though, of course, everyone has their own definitions of these traits. While this short list is by no means exhaustive, there are few parents anywhere who would admit they did not want their children to be happy, healthy and successful, so we will use that limited idea here. There are many ways that adults can actually think about how to support their children's development, including:

- When faced with a child who refuses to eat meat,

consider asking the question differently. Instead of saying: "my child won't eat meat—what do I do?" Ask: "How can I support my child eating a healthy plant-based diet?"

- Consider significantly reducing or totally eliminating animal products from your diet. Raise your children vegan. There are many reasons and resources to do so:
  - **Human health:** Eating a whole food plant-based diet has been scientifically proven to improve human health, reduce or reverse chronic illness, stop or cure some cancers—the issue is settled, plants are better than animals as food for humans. (See: *Forks Over Knives, What the Health, The Game Changers, The China Study, How Not to Die...*)
  - **Global warming:** Ending animal agriculture is the fastest way to mitigating and stabilizing our climate in order to give us the time to transition to sustainable energy sources and save life on earth.
  - **Stopping mass species extinctions:** Ending animal agriculture is the only way to stop the destruction of habitats and restore biodiversity.
  - **Creating social justice:** Animal agriculture

accounts for 18% of human calories consumed, yet uses 45% of arable land and mass amounts of water and fossil fuels to create. Currently 7% of arable land is used to grow all plant food consumed by humans or 82% of total calories consumed. We can end hunger and go a long way to end global poverty by eating a plant based diet.

- **Creating compassion, evidencing a huge reduction in violence:** There are currently 70 billion land animals killed every year for human food and trillions of sea animals killed every year. The amount of violence humans visit on animals is truly incomprehensible. And that violence does not just happen over there, or behind closed doors. Our friends, family and neighbors are forced to participate in unbelievable cruelty and that cruelty finds its way into our cultures, our communities, our homes. We can do better.

- **Reducing prejudices towards other humans:** It appears to be true that devaluing non-human animals allows us to think differently about groups of people who are different from us, allowing us to discriminate against them. In one intriguing study, people who were taught that animals are more like humans than different from them, also had more empathy and compassion for immigrants. [18]

- Pause when your child does something that you don't expect, and think about the meaning behind the action:
  - refusing to eat meat or drink milk
  - crying when they learn the nugget on their plate used to be a live chicken
  - not wanting to wear leather shoes or sit on leather furniture
  - wanting to save the injured bird or small mammal or insect
  - showing empathy to other species

  How can you respond in a way that supports your child to express their thoughts and emotions in a respectful manner, even if their beliefs do not align with yours? What would this take? What might the outcome be—for you, your child and our culture?

  There are many programs around the world to support parents and teachers in teaching children in more humane ways—see the Humane Education Program by Mercy for

Animals and a list of more options at Sentient-Media.org [19]

- Plant a native garden, even if only a 10' x 2' area along a fence or building. Adding native plants will bring in butterflies, hummingbirds, songbirds and other small animals and insects and teach you and the kids about the awesomeness of life on earth. And check out Home Grown National Park to become part of the movement to restore biodiversity one planting at a time.
- Think about your own learning in these areas.
    - How did you learn where food comes from?
    - What did you think about that at the time? Did you experience any trauma? How do you think that impacted your life?
- Share your stories with us (and your childrens' stories) so that others can gain insight and courage to act differently: gamebpress.com

We all know that children should be taken seriously. Children develop in a myriad of ways—physically, psychologically, emotionally, intellectually, spiritually—and each of these areas are important to their overall sense of wellbeing as individuals and as members of communities.

Nurturing a child's natural empathy and compassion is an important part of their overall development. Biophilia, our natural interest in and empathy for other living beings and

THE INVITATION

the natural world should be embraced and expanded upon. Supporting children to eat a vegan diet and live a vegan lifestyle seems to be a great place to start.

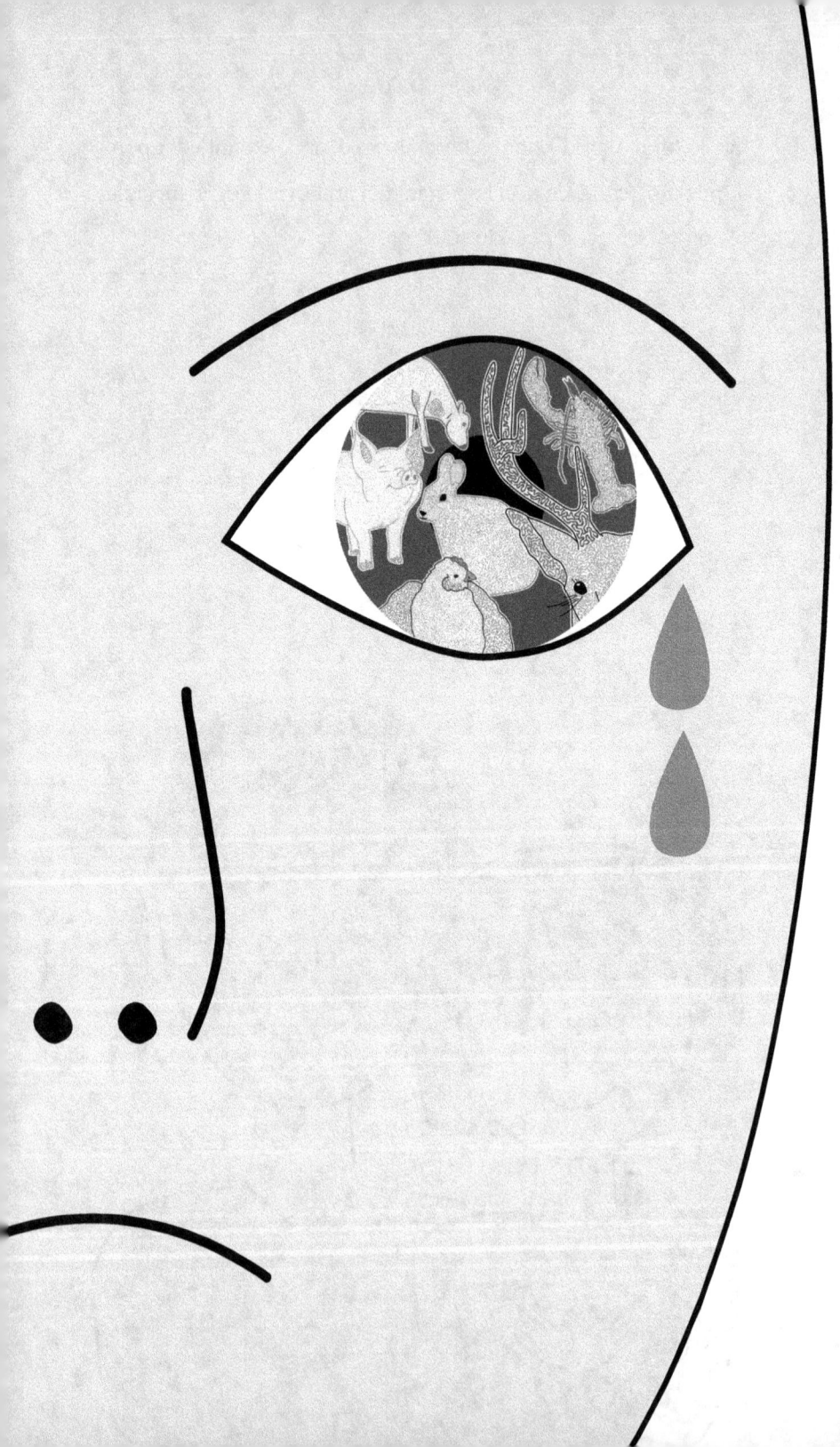

Conclusion

Humans tend to think that we are not animals. That concept, in and of itself, causes us a great deal of difficulty.

We believe that other animals live fundamentally different lives than our own, though the evidence, both scientifically and experientially, paints a much different picture. While there are many differences between human cultures and non-human cultures, there are also many, many similarities. The similarities are much more important than the differences.

And there are major differences between human cultures, yet we fully understand that all humans are human. (We still assign more value to some and that is another concept that causes huge problems for us but is not the topic of this book.)

All of us—including all types of animals, including mammals, birds, fish, amphibians, crustaceans, insects— communicate with each other, build or find shelter, find or cultivate food, procreate, raise their children, deal with injury and illness and mourn their dead. The fact that ALL beings do not do these things *in the exact same way* does not mean that they don't do these things.

Why we began to believe this is something of a mystery, though it appears to have occurred at the time we began to enslave animals (by herding them together) and use them widely for our own purposes. Perhaps this belief made it easier to commit atrocities against them.

The cruelty of forcing living beings to do the things we want them to do, stealing their children, taking their milk or eggs or honey and ultimately taking their lives for our own purposes has always been atrocious. However, the level of cruelty has exponentially expanded with the advent of slaughterhouses, confined animal feeding operations (CAFOs), artificial insemination, forced feedings, and factory farming. Factory farming has moved much of the work inside massive buildings, where the animals suffer alone and the work cannot be seen.

These atrocities cause many problems for humans. It is difficult to find workers to work in these conditions, so companies rely on illegal immigrants and current or former felons as laborers, people who have difficulty finding other work and who do not have the protection to complain. Slaughterhouses and CAFOs are mostly situated in poor, rural communities, out of sight from most of society where they can pollute freely and carry out cruelty behind walls.

The impact of this cruelty is felt much farther than the animals, as explored by Fitzgerald, Kalof, and Dietz in *Slaughterhouses and Increased Crime Rates: An Empirical Analysis of the*

CONCLUSION

Spillover From "The Jungle" Into the Surrounding Community:

> "...slaughterhouse employment increases total arrest rates, arrests for violent crimes, arrests for rape, and arrests for other sex offenses in comparison with other industries. This suggests the existence of a 'Sinclair effect' unique to the violent workplace of the slaughterhouse, a factor that has not previously been examined in the sociology of violence." [20]

We even have laws forbidding people from taking photos or videos of the work and sharing them. Animal rights workers trying to bring the reality to public view are considered terrorists. Terrorists! How is that even possible?

An article from The University of Adelaide takes a historical look at our belief in our differences from and superiority over other animals:

> "'For millennia, all kinds of authorities—from religion to eminent scholars—have been repeating the same idea ad nauseam, that humans are exceptional by virtue that they are the smartest in the animal kingdom,' says Dr Arthur Saniotis, Visiting Research Fellow with the University's School of Medical Sciences. 'However, science tells us that animals can have cognitive faculties that are superior to human beings.'
>
> He says the belief that humans have superior

intelligence harks back to the Agricultural Revolution some 10,000 years ago when people began producing cereals and domesticating animals. This gained momentum with the development of organised religion, which viewed human beings as the top species in creation." [21]

We have a belief that humans are different from and superior to other animals, while we have an abundance of scientific evidence that we are much more alike in all the ways that actually matter. And this belief of human exceptionalism is widely linked to the belief in organized religion. We are holding beliefs built on a foundation of beliefs while discounting scientific evidence and our own personal experiences and observations. It's time to seriously reevaluate our belief systems.

Humans have used all of the following traits or abilities to claim that only humans do these things and that these things "prove" that humans are exceptional, better than, different from other animals:

- Opposable thumbs
- Use of tools
- Solving problems
- Experiencing emotions
- Building shelters
- Having sex for fun and in multiple ways
- Having family relationships, raising children
- Mourning the dead

As it turns out, none of these things are restricted to humans. They apply to many animals, maybe most, if we knew how to see and understand living beings. How many times do we have to make the same mistake?

The underlying desire to believe in our uniqueness is explored by Chapman and Huffman in *Why do we want to think humans are different?*:

> "These and many other such claims about putative defining differences between humans and animals span from 1833 to 2014 have proved wrong. Yet the desire to see humans as unique still remains. Is this a valid scientific question? One of the distinctive features of science is hypothesis testing (Cartmill, 1990; Popper, 1968). If hypotheses about human uniqueness repeatedly prove to be wrong for one trait after another, does this not imply that the hypothesis itself is wrong? We can keep resurrecting the hypothesis with new traits not yet considered, but to what end?" [22]

To what end indeed? We are all alike. And yes, that means we have to change our behavior. Changing behavior is difficult, though not impossible. And it appears that humans are born with the empathy to see other animals as living beings worthy of love, compassion and respect. Supporting those natural tendencies in our children can move us a long way to changing our behavior in a generation. Perhaps we will be returning to our natural behavior.

It is also interesting to contemplate that human exceptionalism appears to be based on very limited qualities. The only things noted to be of value are things that humans obviously have. I would posit that:

- flying,
- being able to breathe underwater,
- great strength,
- the ability to regrow limbs,
- the ability to hibernate and significantly slow down your metabolism,
- the ability to metamorphose,
- echolocation,
- navigating without maps,

and perhaps many other abilities are also "exceptional"!

Yet, none of those make the list. Huh? Interesting. It's kinda fun when you get to write all the rules, but that doesn't make those rules correct, ethical or even real. And these beliefs have caused a great deal of problems for everyone, including humans. So no one species has ALL the exceptional qualities. Yet all those qualities are exceptional and humans have spent a lot of time, energy and resources to figure out how to copy them however we can and however artificially.

We even had to make sure the idea of rights only applied to humans and we label them at every turn—**human rights**. It is time to think about **living rights** rather than human rights. All the rights we currently hold for humans should apply to every

CONCLUSION

living being including some who are not sentient. Think clean and abundant water, fresh air, a home (soil), the freedom to live.

Fixed Mindsets & Growth Mindsets

Our capacity to change is affected by our mindset — Carol Dweck's research on fixed vs. growth mindsets shows that children who are encouraged to have a growth mindset are more likely to exhibit honesty and challenge themselves to improve. [23]

Institutionalising these beliefs of human supremacy is literally and actively destroying life on earth. The earth will survive. But humans will not stay here nor will thousands of other species. We are destroying life on earth. There already is and will continue to be unbelievable levels of pain and suffering if our current behavior continues. All because some people adopted and spread a belief that humans are better than the remainder of the living planet. And almost all of us bought into it to one degree or another. It's time to rethink our beliefs.

Science does not support human supremacy. We now have proof of the sentience of non human beings. We have proof of animal intelligence. We have proof of animal communication and culture. We know that many others recognize themselves, use tools, solve problems, have long lasting relationships…

Experience does not support human supremacy. We all have personal and collective experiences that tell us that other animals think and have emotions like us—think of the whale that carried her dead baby for days. The dog who went to the train station for years waiting for his human to return. Elephant funerals. The robin parents who help their children learn to fly. The geese who stay together for life. The lobster who holds the claw of another when they relocate. There are too many examples to list. How many examples do we really need?

All life is exceptional. And beautiful. And worth protecting. And our children are born knowing this. We know this.

Why do we take something as beautiful as the love and empathy a child is born with, and turn it into something obscene and perverse? Taking the lives of others for our own pleasure—for food, clothing, furniture, entertainment, research—however we use animals, certainly meets the definitions of obscene and perverse. And yes, there may have been a time when humans had to or believe they had to use animals in order to survive. But we no longer need to use animals in any way for any purpose and the fact that we continue to do so, with everything we know today, is truly astonishing. Is this really the future we want our children to inherit?

Think about this.

Our relationship with animals is horrifically wrong. It has gotten totally out of control, obscene and perverse to an unimaginable level. Animal agriculture (for the purpose of eating or using animal body parts), animal genocide (to prevent animals

CONCLUSION

from disrupting human agriculture or human enjoyment of the outdoors or to get rid of excess domestic animals or the animals perceived to disrupt our own animal genocide), and animal kidnapping (for medicine, research, entertainment, black market companion animals) is literally causing the sixth largest mass extinction on earth.

It has taken huge volcanoes, meteors and other spectacular events to cause the first five mass extinctions, but humans are causing the sixth, and largely due to our horrifically wrong relationship with animals and the natural world.

Let's raise the next generation of human children to know the truth and act like they do. Because they are born knowing this and they deserve to live their lives in a peaceful compassionate world—as do all children of all species.

I Knew When I Was Five
(the poem)

I knew when I was five
And no one had to tell me.
That killing is wrong.

That every life is precious no matter who it is,
or what color, shape, size—or species—
he or she or they happen to be.

———

Lobsters have complex lives.

The women choose whose babies they will have and
mothers carry their eggs for 9 to 11 months
before they are born.

Lobsters grow old and wise and can live 100 years
and grow 3 feet long and weigh 40 pounds.

I knew when I was five and no one had to tell me
that boiling a 1-pound, 5-year-old lobster alive
to satisfy human tastebuds
was wrong.

———

CONCLUSION

Rabbits are gregarious and live in communities
of up to 100 individuals.

They build houses underground together
with separate rooms for living and sleeping
and make lifelong friends who play together,
calm each other when stressed,
and nurture each other when sick.

I knew when I was eight and no one had to tell me
that killing and skinning 40 rabbits
so that one human can wear a fur coat
was wrong.

———

Chickens are proud and inquisitive
and live in large, stable social groups.
They feel joy and fear and are very curious.
Chickens are good mothers
whose wings protect their babies.

I knew when I was twelve and no on had to tell me
that killing and cooking the chickens from next door
— the very individuals who came through the fence
to play with my horse —
was wrong.

———

Cows are gentle giants,
contemplative, collaborative, and compassionate.
They form lifelong friendships,
enjoy intellectual challenges,
and jump for joy when they solve a problem.

I knew when I was sixteen and no had to tell me
that making friends with a calf
— playing with her, caring for her,
bathing and grooming her for the 4-H show —
only to kill her, dismember her, and eat her
was wrong.

———————

Pigs are smart enough to play video games
against chimpanzees and win.
Pigs are peaceful, rarely show anger
and are very kind to each other.

I knew when I was twenty and no one had to tell me
that "celebrating" with co-workers while a
teenage pig with an apple wedged in his mouth
roasted over an open fire
to please our palates
was wrong.

———————

CONCLUSION

Deer are highly social beings
with women living communally,
caring for their infants and children.
Groups of teenage boys hang out together,
finding food and staying safe.
The men are territorial and live a more solitary life.

I knew when I was thirty two and no one had to tell me
that stalking, baiting and shooting unarmed deer
for fun
was wrong.

But someone did have to point out—
even though I disapproved of hunting,
finding it cruel and unnecessary,
every individual deer had a chance
to outrun the arrow or the bullet

while not a single cow or pig or chicken
ever had a chance against the slaughterhouse blade.

I knew when I was five and no one had to tell me.
I knew when I was eight and no one had to tell me.
I knew when I was twelve and no one had to tell me.
I knew when I was sixteen and no one had to tell me.

We Know

I knew when I was twenty and no one had to tell me.
I knew when I was thirty-two. And yet...

the confinement, the torture, the killing,
the eating of sentient beings continues
with numbers so large they are incomprehensible—
70 BILLION a year worldwide.

More animals die for human food each week
than all the humans killed in all the wars
in all of recorded history.

When will we all know enough to stop?

                        And when will the adults support the children
                                      who already know?

CONCLUSION

Visit GameBPress.com:

- for more about *I Knew When I Was Five* and to download coloring pages from the book

- to share your experience with the normalization of violence—did you know, too?

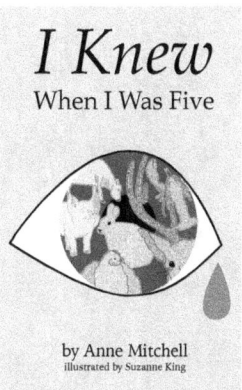

> *I Knew When I Was Five* shares a powerful message and gives a glimpse into experiences many have had growing up in a culture that has normalized eating fellow animals. Kindness and compassion is what is most natural to us. We know at a deep intuitive level that harming fellow beings does not serve us. This book takes you on a journey of that inner knowing that is incredibly precious and important to tap into in order to create a more peaceful world.
>
> — Anna Ferguson, author, *World Peace Yoga*, and Founder, Heärt Montessori

REFERENCES

[1]
A response from Jason Reynolds, the United States' national ambassador for young people's literature, to the question from Stephen Colbert: "what is it you learn from your interaction with your own audience?" on The Late Show with Stephen Colbert, December 2, 2021 on NBC (edited for clarity).

[2]
Definition of "indoctrinate" (oxfordlearnersdictionaries.com/us/definition/english/indoctrinate)

[3]
Definition of "biophilia" (dictionary.cambridge.org/us/dictionary/english/biophilia)

[4]
Description of "livestock" (vocabulary.com/dictionary/livestock)

[5]
How to teach a fish to count
by Philip Ball
(bbc.com/future/article/20130429-how-to-teach-a-fish-to-count)

[6]
How very young children think about animals
by Judy DeLoache, M.B. Pickard, and Vanessa LoBue
(researchgate.net/publication/288024673_How_very_young_children_think_about_animals)

[7]
Reimagining the human
by Eileen Crist
(science.org/doi/abs/10.1126/science.aau6026)

[8]
Cultural Solipsism, Cultural Lenses, Universal Principles, And Animal Advocacy
by Thomas G. Kelch
(animallaw.info/article/cultural-solipsism-cultural-lenses-universal-principles-and-animal-advocacy)

[9]
Timeline of animal welfare and rights, Wikipedia entry
(en.wikipedia.org/wiki/Timeline_of_animal_welfare_and_rights)

[10]
Information about taste buds from Nemours Children's Health (kidshealth.org/en/kids/taste-buds.html)

[11]
Corporate personhood, Wikipedia entry (en.wikipedia.org/wiki/Corporate_personhood)

[12]
Ganges and Yamuna rivers granted same legal rights as human beings
by Michael Safi and agencies
(theguardian.com/world/2017/mar/21/ganges-and-yamuna-rivers-granted-same-legal-rights-as-human-beings)

[13]
This river in New Zealand is legally a person. Here's how it happened
by Julia Hollingsworth
(cnn.com/2020/12/11/asia/whanganui-river-new-zealand-intl-hnk-dst/index.html)

[14]
Toddler Won't Eat Meat? Read This by Amy Palanjian
(yummytoddlerfood.com/why-wont-my-toddler-eat-meat/)

[15]
5 Things To Do When Your Toddler Won't Eat Meat
by Ivana Davies
(findyourmomtribe.com/toddler-wont-eat-meat/)

[16]
4 Tips From A Dietitian To Get Your Child To Eat Meat
(firststepnutrition.com/blog/kidsandmeat/)

[17]
BBC Good Food Nation: Survey looks at children's eating habits
(bbc.co.uk/newsround/58653757)

[18]
The Human-Animal Divide and Prejudices Against Humans
by Gordon Hodson, Ph.D.
(psychologytoday.com/ca/blog/without-predice/201206/the-human-animal-divide-and-prejudices-against-humans)

[19]
Raising Vegans: Parents Counter Big Ag's Influence in the Classroom
by Jessica Scott-Reid
(sentientmedia.org/raised-vegan-parents-counter-big-ags-influence-in-the-classroom/)

[20]
Slaughterhouses and Increased Crime Rates: An Empirical Analysis of the Spillover From "The Jungle" Into the Surrounding Community
by Amy J. Fitzgerald, Linda Kalof, and Thomas Dietz
(journals.sagepub.com/doi/10.1177/1086026609338164)

REFERENCES

[21]
Humans Not Smarter Than Animals, Just Different
by The University of Adelaide
(adelaide.edu.au/news/news67182.html)

[22]
Why do we want to think humans are different?
by Colin A.Chapman and Michael A. Huffman
(wellbeingintlstudiesrepository.org/cgi/viewcontent.cgi?article=1358&context=animsent)

[23]
There are a lot of resources on fixed vs. growth mindsets, including a book by Dweck called *Mindset: The New Psychology of Success*. For some of the peer-reviewed research in childhood development, see: *Implicit Theories of Intelligence Predict Achievement Across an Adolescent Transition: A Longitudinal Study and an Intervention* by Lisa S. Blackwell, Kali H. Trzesniewski, and Carol Sorich Dweck (srcd.onlinelibrary.wiley.com/doi/10.1111/j.1467-8624.2007.00995.x)

WITH GRATITUDE

There are so many individuals to thank for their part in making this book a reality—some who encouraged me, others who challenged me and all ultimately helped me to clarify my thinking, my intent, and my writing.

The non-humans who challenge me to consider their points of view like Beavis, one of the squirrels who lives in the backyard and is very demanding and often vexing; Samantha, the pond goldfish who allowed us into her world as she developed a fatal disease and gave us the opportunity to explore the very small world of fish veterinary care and perhaps to encourage an expansion of that world in our local community; the songbirds, hummingbirds, butterflies and insects who have come to rely on our backyard plantings for their sustenance and shelter; our family dogs, Vino and Niki, who constantly show us their intelligence, humor, grace and character; the individuals who live at our local farmed animal sanctuary (and those at other sanctuaries) who put faces and unique personalities to the barbaric "meat" in our stores and restaurants. All of you encourage, sometimes demand, me to think more deeply and consider the world I actually want to live in.

I am also grateful to everyone who read the work before publication and offered up errors, questions, additional points to consider and encouragement to keep going. I am especially grateful to Laura Pflug, Robert Grillo, Josh Levine, Glen Merzer, and Pamela Wampler. Their insights, questions and ideas were beyond helpful.

This book would not be possible without Suzanne King and Benjamin Kohen. I'm never sure how to label Suzanne—writing partner, illustrator, editor, IT support, muse—the list is endless. I adore working with Suzanne; she is such an inspiration.

And my husband Chuck Shuman. I don't even have the words to tell him how much his support means to me. Without his patience, understanding and willingness to discuss things for hours at a time, there would be no written work.

With enormous gratitude—thank you all!

www.ingramcontent.com/pod-product-compliance
Lightning Source LLC
Chambersburg PA
CBHW070924080526
44589CB00013B/1426